*In memory of my mother Nell Courtis Player*
*(née Pearce)*

who danced with
Leonard Keddell (60)
in Mevagissey

with thanks for
many happy hours
at Bodrugan
from Pennie (Doctor)
Mevagissey
28.9.08

# MASTER MARINER

## CAPTAIN WALTER WILLIAMS
### 1806–1882
### *Of Mevagissey*

## PENNIE DENTON

PEVERIL PRESS 2008

Map of Mevagissey area showing the family homes of the Williams and Pearces: Tregerrick, Trelawney and the Anchorage

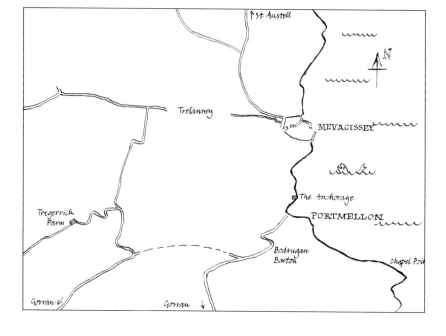

*Between pp.5 & 6:*
The *Brilliant* of Mevagissey, *c.*1850, by Michele Funno

Published by Peveril Press
South Barn
Durlston
Swanage BH19 2JG

First published September 2008

Designed by Sheri Gee

Printed in Great Britain by Cambridge University Press, Cambridge

ISBN 978 0 9542790 1 1

# CONTENTS

Mevagissey harbour, *c.*1920. (Nell Pearce)

# *FISHYGISSY*

*After looking at the pier at Mevagissey, we went into the town, but of all the places I ever was in this is the most wretched and disagreeable. In the whole town there seems to be scarcely a habitation fit for a human being to dwell in. The streets were all nauseous and offensive to a great degree. For this was the season of the year for catching pilchards, and during the operation of curing the fish, a very fetid oil arises from them. This constitutes a considerable part of the employment as well as the riches of the inhabitants of this part of Cornwall at this season of the year.*

A GENTLEMAN FROM HAMBLE, HAMPSHIRE, 1793[1]

M Y MOTHER would never eat fish. She said that the stench of the fishermen's catch around the harbour wafted up to Tregoney Hill in Mevagissey, where she was born in 1905, and made her feel so ill that she was put off eating fish for life. Even inland at her grandmother's farm, Tregerrick at Gorran, she could not escape. At Christmas her grandmother used to sell geese and turkeys. Christmas day was ruined for my mother as she was forced to eat fish-flavoured slices of goose; the birds had been fattened up on that local delicacy, the pilchard.

Families in Mevagissey tended to be connected either with the sea or the land, but there was no hard and fast division. My mother's father, Morley Pearce, was a carpenter; his parents were farmers; one of his grandparents was a farmer and the other a master mariner. Many of the village occupations were seasonal, or for a limited

My great-grand-
parents, William
and Jane Pearce
c.1885.

period, so that in between their main work fishermen might help on the farms, and farm
labourers with the fishing. As well as making
coffins and cartwheels, my grandfather kept
cows, a donkey, a horse, pigs, ducks and chick-
ens. He sold milk from a little window at his
house. His mother had refused to let him work
on the family farm at Gorran as he was thought
to be 'delicate'; nevertheless, as well as being a
carpenter and running his small holding, he
built a number of houses including Trelawney
on Tregoney Hill. This impressive Edwardian
villa, with views of the harbour, was built by
him in 1901 for his bride from the Midlands,
Clara Linnett, who had come down from Birmingham to teach at the village school because
she longed to live by the sea.

My grandfather's four brothers and two sisters helped to run the
farm at Tregerrick. Later, some of the boys took on farms of their own
and their sister Jane taught at Gorran School. Granny Pearce, my
mother always maintained, was an 'old basket'. She used to invent
uncongenial tasks for my mother and her brother, Thirlby: idleness
was not permitted when they visited Tregerrick. But my mother found
that she was left alone if she sat on the pile of logs reading, or pretend-
ing to read, religious literature such as *Pilgrim's Progress*.

Granny Pearce always dressed in black, brushed her hair a hundred
times every morning and was a strict Methodist. But she lacked warmth
and kindness and seems to have been always more concerned with her
own needs, and perceived religious standards, than the needs of others.
Her lively, pretty daughter Annie was ordered to stop seeing her
boyfriend, indeed never to marry, as she was needed on the farm. Perhaps Granny Pearce's harshness had contributed to the terrible day in
1889 when her husband, William, threw himself down a well on the
farm. Or, perhaps, more charitably, it may be that the loss of her husband had made her hard as she struggled to manage the farm and seven
children on her own.

\*

*Above*: Tregerrick, Gorran. Clara Pearce, my grandmother, is sitting on the lawn, *c.*1900
*Below*: Morley Pearce on his small holding at Trelawney

Trelawney,
Tregoney Hill,
Mevagissey. Built
by my grandfather,
Morley Pearce,
for his wife, Clara
Linnett

When the Second World War broke out my parents were living in Southampton and, fearing that the area was vulnerable to enemy attack, they decided that my mother and I, then a baby of 3 months, would be safer in Cornwall with her family. My grandfather had died the year before I was born and my mother always regretted that he never saw me, as he loved children. He, in turn, was much loved by family and friends and respected in the village. I recall my grandmother as a picture-book grandmother with white hair and a kind face. A schoolmistress from the rather more progressive Midlands, she was independent and headstrong; the first person to own a bicycle in Mevagissey (but why one would want one in such a hilly little town I cannot imagine) and one of the few inhabitants never to attend church or chapel. This was not because she was an atheist or an agnostic but because she was a Baptist and there was no Baptist chapel in Mevagissey.

My memories of staying at Trelawney on Tregoney Hill are hazy as I was only five when my grandmother died and the house was sold. But I do remember the long, long trek up the hill from the shops and having to wait patiently as my grandmother and mother stopped to chat to everyone they met on the way up. One day, clinging to my mother's hand, I remember being squeezed together with a great crowd of people in one of the little alleys between Fore Street and the quay, straining to look at what was going on around the harbour. It seems that we were attempting to see Johnny Frenchman, the eponymous hero of the 1945 Ealing film, strutting about the harbour, part of which had been transformed into a Breton port; but perhaps we were hoping to become extras in the film. I remember feeling a bit threatened by the tall people pressing against me but the filming must have provided welcome entertainment for the little town after the long, sad days of war. I saw the film recently and was as appalled by the wooden acting

and laughable mock-Cornish accents as I was enthralled by the glimpses of Mevagissey as it looked in 1945.

Shelling peas with my grandmother at Trelawney, *c*.1940

\*

After my grandmother died in 1945 Trelawney was sold and we no longer visited Cornwall. Then in 1959, when I was at university, my mother suggested I drive her down to Mevagissey to visit her Aunt Annie. We found the harbour little changed; still filled with fishing boats, surrounded by drying nets and fishing gear and fishermen in Guernsey smocks sitting on up-turned lobster pots putting the world to rights. There was a lingering smell of fish, and gulls wheeled and cried to each other across the water. My mother asked a couple of fishermen sitting on fish boxes if they minded if I took a photograph of them. They surveyed us silently for a while, then one said to my mother, "Baint you Morley Pearce's daughter, Nellie?' She admitted that she was and they began an enjoyable and interminable chat about the old Mevagissey families; the Clokes, the Dunns, the Pollards and so on. Throughout the nineteenth and twentieth centuries the population of Mevagissey remained constant at around 2,000; just the size for most people to know each other. Without realising it we had arrived on the day of the famous Floral Dance and in the evening we found ourselves

Fishermen on the Quay at Mevagissey, 1959 (Pennie Denton)

linking arms and dancing along the narrow streets meeting more and more people who seemed to know my mother and her family.

The next day we visited Great-Aunt Annie, my grandfather's sister, who had moved from the family farm in Gorran to St Austell after the death of her mother. She was the one who had not been allowed by

Granny Pearce to marry, as she was needed on the farm. Everyone loved Aunt Annie and her house was the first place for family members who had left Cornwall to visit and enjoy her warm interest in their lives, and her traditional cream teas.

Great-Aunt Annie's front room was dominated by an unexpectedly large and vivid painting of a ship in full sail entering a harbour (see between pp. 5 & 6 and front cover). In the background billowing clouds, tinged with yellow and white, rose up from an erupting volcano, masking its flames, which cast a pink glow across the sky. It could only be Naples. The image of the ship sailing into the Italian port, bow waves breaking on a calm, ultramarine sea, conjured up warm climates and adventure. In the foreground three fishermen on a rock watch the ship as she sails by. One of them raises his hand perhaps to indicate the fine sight to his friends, or perhaps to wave to the captain who looks back impassively. Six sailors, wearing hats, can just be seen above the gunwale, inactive except for one who is busily hauling up a huge red banner. It flutters from the top of the mast with the single word 'BRILLIANT' emblazoned upon it. A caption underneath the painting identified the ship as the 'BRILLIANT OF MEVAGISSEY'. I wish I could reproduce Aunt Annie's Cornish accent when she told me that the master of this romantic-looking ship had been her grandfather and my great-great- grandfather, Captain Walter Langford Williams. 'He were a bit of an old pirate,' she said. And that was it – for the time being. She was born in 1875 and he died in 1882 when she was 7, so she must have known him. Her mother, the fearsome Granny Pearce, was his first child. How I wish I had asked her more.

The painting of the *Brilliant* had stimulated my curiosity and a thousand questions sprang to mind. Did the ship really sail all the way from Mevagissey to Naples? Why would it go there? Who exactly was Captain Walter Williams? At this stage I knew nothing of my mother's family and it wasn't until she was in her nineties that I began to ask her questions about them. She drew up a rough family tree headed, rather mysteriously, as follows:

Capt. Williams – owner of sailing ships
'Anchorage'
£50 in 1820, £500 in 1850

13

# 1

# THE SEARCH

*Most objects rot, are discarded, or get lost. Others lose their history, which is their very meaning. With each day, old homes are abandoned and forebears' memories fade. And with them goes all that has ever happened until we realise what we have lost, and the archives are full of us, armed with threadbare family trees, hunting down the past as if to make ourselves complete by it.*

JEREMY SEAL, *The Wreck at Sharpnose Point*[1]

THE ARMY of us searching for our ancestors know only too well the 'brick wall' beyond which we can find nothing and so are left floundering in speculation or imagination. First there is that 'threadbare family tree' and then the attempt to fill it out; to find out just who these people were, where they lived and what they did and thought. But, sadly, unless the family is educated and probably well born the family tree will remain bare. Only surviving written words in the form of letters and diaries, and visual records such as paintings and photographs, can enable us to get any real insight into their lives. Most poor people were illiterate and few wrote letters or diaries or left anything that can tell us today what kind of people they were. Although many official records (court records, census records, customs' records, records from government departments, parliamentary records and so on) survive from the eighteenth and nineteenth centuries they rarely reveal more than a few more dates for the family tree. Even the recent past eludes us.

When my parents died, as their only child I inevitably inherited a number of objects. Many of them had indeed 'lost their history' for I had no idea where they had come from. I knew that the sale and emptying of my grandmother's house in Mevagissey, Trelawney, had been a hurried affair as she died in February 1945 when war was still making travel difficult. Somehow, in the transfer, things were lost including my grandmother's photograph albums. However, I have inherited amongst other things an octant, a model of a steam sailing ship in a wooden case with a glass front and a print of Portmellon from the *Illustrated London News* of 1849. Other members of the family have also inherited objects from our common ancestors, including the painting of the *Brilliant* which I had seen at Aunt Annie's house in St Austell and a ceramic punch bowl decorated with a picture of a sailing ship in a foreign harbour.

I decided to start my search in Mevagissey churchyard. It seemed grimly appropriate that the rain was lashing down as I made my way to the church and wandered around peering at the stone and slate gravestones. Cornish churchyards are full of the exquisitely lettered and decorated slate stones from the eighteenth century and earlier. I turned left up a grassy bank just inside the churchyard gate and began my search. Almost immediately, under a huge beech tree near the gate, I found what I was looking for. The memorial was in stone, not slate, and was 'In affectionate remembrance of Ann, the beloved wife of Walter Langford Williams of Portmellon, who died March 26, 1869 in her 61st year'. The first word, 'In', was carved in a large gothic script and the rest in a mixture of italic and roman scripts with Ann's name in capitals. Along the rounded top of the stone were the words 'I know

My inheritance: octant, ship model and print of Portmellon during the cholera outbreak of 1849 (Carlotta Barrow)

In
ANN,
Walter Langford Williams
Who died March 26th 1869
"Looking unto Jesus"
WALTER L. WILLIAMS
WHO DIED AT PORTMELLON
21ST OCT. 1882
ALSO
SOPHIA SUSAN
AGED 42 YEARS

that my redeemer liveth' and, underneath, the words 'Looking unto Jesus'. There were two later commemorations in less elegant scripts to 'Walter L. Williams who died at Portmellon 21st Oct. 1882 aged 70' and 'Sophia Susan, wife of Philip Samuel Allen, and daughter of the above, died July 25 1892 aged 42 years. He liveth his beloved sleep'.

*Opposite*: Grave-
stone of Ann, Walter
and Sophia Williams
in Mevagissey
churchyard

It happens that a distant cousin of my mother's, Sophy Tatchell, lives near me in Dorset. I always enjoy talking to Sophy. She was a teacher and headmistress and although she is over ninety, her mind is clear and her memory sharp and she enjoys a busy social life with friends of all ages. Like my mother she is a great-granddaughter of Captain Williams and I thought that she might be able to tell me a little more about the family. I took a photograph of the gravestone to show her. 'Oh,' she said, 'Sophia? I always thought she was called Sophy, like me. That's my grandmother. She was the fourth daughter of Captain Walter and his wife, Ann. They had Jane, Elizabeth, Anne, and then the only boy, Walter, and finally Sophy or Sophia. My grand-mother and her older sister, Elizabeth, married two brothers, William and Philip Allen from Devonport. All went well to start with and both families had several children but then, the story goes, the brothers went off to London and their families never heard from them again – except for one postcard.' They say you should set off in search of your family history with a stout heart and so, for the moment, I ignored this shattering confidence and asked her if she knew where Captain Walter had lived in Portmellon. 'At the Anchorage of course,' she said. 'In the 60s it was brought back into the family by my cousin, Sam Allen, but I hear it's a B & B now. When you next go down to Mevagissey you must look up Sam's daughter, Sue. She married Brian Mitchell, son of the famous Portmellon boatbuilder, Percy Mitchell. I think they live in Mevagissey.'

I woke early and lay listening to the waves breaking on the rocks below just as Captain Walter Williams must have heard them a century and a half ago. The Anchorage is perched high above the sea, with just a small patch of garden alongside a precipitous cliff edge. Looking towards the east, the rising sun dazzled and shimmered on the sea with the headland of the Gribbin silhouetted on the horizon, and to the west was the fairytale outline of Chapel Point. It could not have been more beautiful. Perhaps the Captain had had a telescope up there to watch the merchant ships and fishing fleet come and go. I could only

see one vessel now, a single fishing boat slowly chugging its way into Mevagissey harbour.

I telephoned Sue Mitchell. She was amazed to hear that I was staying at the Anchorage and 'yes' she said, she would come down straight away. She had not been to the house since it had been sold after her father's death in the 1990s and although she did not know a great deal about its history she would love to see it again. When she and Brian arrived we stood outside in the car park space to the east of the house. 'Look,' she said, 'that old hut is where the Captain kept his donkey, and over the road, that old stone building, that was on his land. In fact the field stayed in the family, with the Dunns, who inherited it, and they have only recently sold it.' She explained to me that after Captain Walter's death, the house had been lived in by his only son, Walter, and his wife, who was always known in the family as 'Aunt Pem'. They did not have any children of their own but adopted May Rice, who was an orphan. May married Matthias Dunn and after the death of Walter and Pem, they inherited the house. I was familiar with the names of the Dunns' three daughters, Maisie, Marjorie and Dorothy, as they had been contemporaries and friends of my mother. They feature in her photograph albums, posing on the

*Above, right*: The Anchorage, Portmellon. *Above, left*: The old donkey hut at the Anchorage

local beaches in the glamorous, but modest, costumes of the 1920s.

Sue Mitchell told me that her father, Sam Allen, had bought the Anchorage in about 1964. At first the family used it for holidays but in 1968 they moved there. Sue found the Anchorage very little changed since she and her brother John had sold it after their father's death in the 1990s. The east side of the house, with sloping floors and beams, had probably not changed much since the Captain's time. In the main living room Sue pointed to a painting on what looked as if it might have been a chimney-breast and said to the present owners, Pat and Dermot Lee, 'There used to be an alcove there with a statue of a fisher-girl in it.' Pat lifted up the picture and showed us the alcove. 'And,' she said, 'we have the statue.' She disappeared and returned with the brightly painted statue, about fourteen inches high, of a young girl with a shawl over her head and shoulders and basket in her hand. Could this be another of those objects that connected us to our past? Something else which connected Sue Mitchell and me to Captain Williams and to Mevagissey's past history as a thriving fishing port?

I should point out that until I started searching for Captain Walter, I had never met Sue. But her father, Sam, and Sam's sister, Betty, as well

*Left*: The fisher-girl. *Right*: Betty Allen, my mother's cousin, Stella, a friend from Mevagissey and my mother

as being cousins had been close friends of my mother and her brother, Thirlby, when they were young. Friends and relations of my grandparents, many of them from my grandmother's hometown of Birmingham, would regularly spend holidays with the Pearce family, either at their house, Trelawney, or in lodgings in Mevagissey and Portmellon. My grandfather built a tennis court on some land he had at Portmellon and, as well as enjoying tennis, the visitors would make up cricket teams and play the locals. My mother's family albums are full of photographs of beach and cliff picnics, games on the beach, swimming and boating.

I asked Sue what she knew about the painting of the *Brilliant* that I had seen in Aunt Annie's house. 'Well, when Aunt Annie died in 1972 she left it to my father, Sam, and as we were living at the Anchorage then, it came here. It was hung over there,' she said, indicating the long wall in the living room. 'Dad left it to us, my brother John and me, and as I don't have any children and he does I thought it better for John to have it. So it's up in Derbyshire now. But you don't imagine, do you, that Captain Williams ever went to Naples? Artists just used to paint in any background the captain wanted when they painted their ships.' This was a challenge; did he really go to Naples or was the setting in the picture a fake? I longed to see the painting again; after all, I had only seen it once, briefly, over forty years ago. At Sue's suggestion I wrote to her brother, John, and he kindly arranged to get the painting photographed and I was able to acquire a full-size copy.

What had Jeremy Seal said of the thousands of people like us who are striving to find out something about their ancestors; 'hunting down the past as if to make ourselves complete'? I did not think that was my motive. I was intrigued by the painting of the *Brilliant* and its owner and determined to find out whether they had really sailed all the way from Cornwall to Naples and why. And, yes, perhaps I may have felt that having such an adventurous ancestor might reflect on me, although I doubted if I had inherited any of Walter Williams' characteristics except perhaps a love of the sea. But then sailors often did not love the sea at all.

It was time to do some serious research and I decided to spend the next day at the County Record Office. Those who scoff at train spotters will surely laugh behind their hands at a person who is happiest in a record office or library chasing that elusive reference or frantically netting in red herrings. Red herrings are my speciality. On the rare occasions that my husband has accompanied me on a research trip to Cornwall his logical mind has rejected all those fascinating, but irrelevant, leads and enjoined me to 'stick to the facts'.

So, what are the facts? Children studying history are taught the value of 'evidence'. But just how reliable is 'evidence'? It is alarming how very often those apparently accurate 'facts' are just plain wrong. I have to confess something truly reprehensible. I think of myself as a historian, a seeker after the truth of historical events, but I have, through carelessness, created a lie for future historians of my family. On the beautiful stone I commissioned for my parents' grave, I gave the sculptor the wrong dates. My father was born in 1904 and my mother in 1905; on the stone it says that they were born in 1905 and 1906 respectively.

The records of the nineteenth century provide a rich vein for family historians. To administer a great Empire you needed to know who and what you were dealing with. So, people were counted and their jobs, ages and place of birth noted. The Census after 1841 gives place of residence, occupation, name, age and position in the family. And in the maritime world a plethora of new records was created. Lloyd's Register of Ships, which was started in 1764, gave details of merchant ships including the tonnage and measurements, the ship's builder and place of build, owner and master and main voyages in the year. Lloyd's List gave information on the movement of ships engaged in foreign trade. The Registration of Ships was made compulsory in 1786 and overseen by the Board of Customs. Ships had to be surveyed for seaworthiness and every detail of their size, ownership and demise noted. In 1835 the Merchant Shipping Act was passed to create a central register of all seamen in order to provide support for the Royal Navy in wartime. Before setting out on a voyage the ship's master had to fill in various forms; the most informative of these is the Crew Agreement which was a detailed contract between crew member and employer and lists his name, age, place of birth, date of joining and leaving the ship and the voyages made. All this became part of the apparatus of the state where previously almost the only records of a person's life were the church's, of baptisms, marriages and burials.

Unfortunately, at this time the spelling of names was by no means standardised and as the majority of people could not read and write, names on Census returns and church records vary enormously. I found the name Jennifer, for example, appearing on different documents as Jenifer, Jenefer, Jenepher, Jenupher, Jenny and, somewhat confusingly, just plain Jane. Accuracy was not a priority for seamen either; many were illiterate anyway and could only sign the Crew Lists with a cross. The spelling of their names is often difficult to read, and even more difficult to guess, and their ages and places of birth, too, are often wrongly given.

In the Record Office I thought I would start with the church records and see what I could discover about Walter Langford Williams. From the gravestone I had noted down that he had died on 21 October 1882 aged 70, which meant that he had been born in 1812. I searched through 1812 with no success and then five years either side, still drawing a blank. I was about to give up when I found him. He had been baptised, not in 1812 as I had deduced from the gravestone, but on 10 January 1807. I looked again at the gravestone and realised that 'age 70' was in fact 'age 76' – I had wasted a lot of time searching for the wrong date of birth. However, it had been worth the effort because the record revealed something else; it showed that Walter's father was called Philip, was a mariner, and that his wife was called Jenifer. This was one of those moments when one feels like standing up and disrupting the peace of the other researchers with a shout of triumph; 'Look everyone, I have found my great-great-great-grandparents!'

Exciting as this was, I felt I needed to fill in a bit of background and headed for the Courtney Library at the Royal Institution of Cornwall. Here I found a most wonderfully helpful librarian who indicated an index to something called the Mapplebeck collection. It turned out that the Reverend A. Mapplebeck had been the Vicar of Mevagissey in the 1950s. He must have had a lot of spare time for he had carefully copied out practically every historical reference to Mevagissey that he could find. This was truly a gold mine and from his notes I was able to begin to understand the kind of place Mevagissey had been in the nineteenth century when Captain Walter was alive.

# 2

# PILCHARDS AND PROSPERITY

*One may say that 1775 was the beginning of a new or modern Mevagissey.*

J. HARRIS[1]

IN THE EARLY nineteenth century the harbour area of Mevagissey was busy as men and women with carts bustled about collecting and delivering to ships and fish cellars and shops. Fishermen discussed the weather and the world as they mended nets and prepared their boats; gulls hovered and screeched as they swooped on the fish refuse lying around. There was a strong and persistent smell of fish and tar hovering over the little town. The 2,000 people of Mevagissey, isolated as they were between hills and cliffs and with only rough access roads unfit for carriages, relied on the sea not only for their livelihood but also for communication. Ships calling in from Falmouth, Plymouth, London, or further afield, brought goods for the shops, the fishermen, the ship-building industry, the merchants and

Mevagissey fishermen landing pilchards, 1906 (S. Dalby-Smith)

the people. They also brought news of the world outside Mevagissey and the progress of the war with Napoleon.

The sea provided a living not only for fishermen, sailors and smugglers but also for the men and women working on shore supplying rope, sails, ironwork and blocks to the flourishing local ship-building industry or preparing the fish and fish oil, which was known, curiously, as train oil, for sale. The cottages of the people were adapted to the needs of fishing with storage for nets, tackle, baskets and barrels. In the narrow streets of the town general merchants, who sold everything from fishing nets and salt, to trousers and dresses, corn and sugar, were beginning to be superseded by specialist drapers, grocers and ironmongers. In the surrounding countryside agricultural labourers scraped a living, perpetually on the borderline of pauperism.

For centuries the most important catch in Mevagissey had been the pilchard, which was found only along the south Cornish and Irish coasts and the north coast of Brittany. John Taylor, visiting Cornwall in 1649, was told that 'in the little town of Mevagissey, there are 44 fisher boats, which do fish for pilchards, that every boat hath 6 men and every 2 boats had one net between them: they do call the 2 boats a seine; so there are 22 seines, and 22 nets.'[2] There was only a limited demand for fish at home and the Cornish fishermen depended for their livelihood upon the need for fish on fast days in Italy and the other Catholic countries of the Mediterranean. It is said that the Cornish used to raise their glasses to toast the Pope:

> Here's a Health to the Pope! May he live to repent
> And add just six months to the term of his Lent,
> And tell all his vassals from Rome to the Poles
> There's nothing like pilchards for saving their Souls![3]

From the earliest days the fishing industry in Cornwall had been monopolised by the merchants who supplied the capital, marketed the fish overseas and disposed of the industry's valuable by-product, train oil. It was said that to preserve good fish, fit for foreign markets, the pilchards should lie in bulk for three or four weeks, with around three bushels of salt to each hogshead. They should then be pressed for at least three weeks. The large cask used to store dry or liquid goods, known as a hogshead, held 52 gallons or 2,950 pilchards. In a good

fishing season, anything from 20–40,000 hogsheads might be exported.[4] Once packed, the fish were got away as soon as possible in order to avoid the winter storms and because the first consignments usually commanded the highest prices. An average cargo consisted of about 5–600 hogsheads, equal to about 100–120 tons. Because of the shortness of the season and the long round journey, few vessels made more than one trip a year.[5]

In the late eighteenth and early nineteenth centuries Mevagissey experienced a period of great prosperity. There were 60 fishermen registered there in 1775 and in the same year an Act of Parliament was passed for the completion and maintenance of the harbour. Those who subscribed to the fund for building the new pier were the wealthiest and most influential figures in the community. The Duke of Buckingham, who owned about half the land in Mevagissey, subscribed £100, the merchant John Pearce, senior, £100, H.H. Tremayne of Heligan, £50, Thomas Stark, cooper, £50 and the ship-builder Thomas Shepheard, £45. The well-known fish merchants of Falmouth, G.C. Fox & Son, who had interests in Mevagissey, subscribed £20 and £4,235 was raised in total.[6]

When the new harbour was completed it was said to have the best facilities between Plymouth and Falmouth and, according to the journalist J.H. Harris who was a Mevagissey man, its completion had an immediate effect upon the development and fortune of the town; a safe harbour with improved moorings for larger trading vessels and

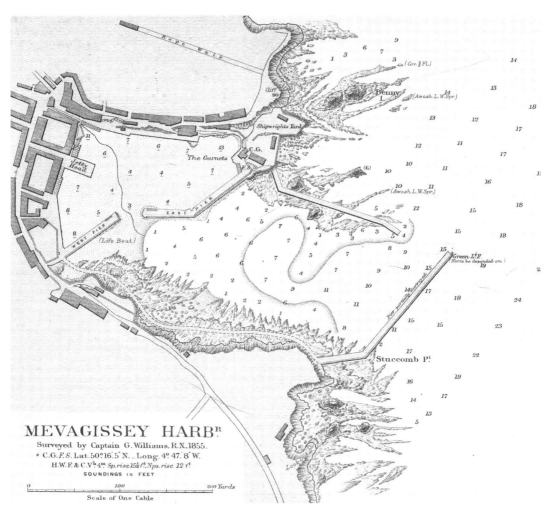

MEVAGISSEY HARB.ᴿ

Surveyed by Captain G. Williams, R.N. 1855.
* C.G.F.S. Lat. 50° 16'.5" N. _ Long. 4° 47'.8" W.
H.W. F. & C. V.ʰ 4ᵐ Sp. rise 15¾ f.ᵗ Nps. rise 12 f.ᵗ
SOUNDINGS ᴵN FEET

0        100        200 Yards
Scale of One Cable

Plan of Mevagissey harbour, 1856. The Rope Walk and Shipwright's Yard are shown at the top of the drawing.

the fishermen meant new opportunities for trading and the traditional fishing industry. Smuggling, privateering, profitable freights and good pilchard seasons enabled many people of the town to accumulate wealth. As capital flowed into the town, new houses and cellars in brick, stone and granite were constructed around the harbour and in the narrow streets behind it.[7] But fishing was always an uncertain livelihood. In good years the catches were enormous and the main problem was getting the fish to those who ate them or the oil produced from them to those who used it. In poor years the cries of the huers, who announced the approach of the shoals of pilchards to the seine owners, were silent as the fish stayed away and many fishermen were reduced to poverty.

The period of prosperity in Mevagissey was brought to an abrupt

26

halt by Napoleon, who forbade all trade between Britain and France, France's allies and the neutral countries from 1806 to 1812. At the end of the war every effort was made by Mevagissey merchants and fishermen to revive their trade. By 1850 there were eighty fishing boats, seines and drifters, registered in Mevagissey, giving employment to over three hundred fishermen, packers, bulkers and carriers. There were ten fish-curing businesses and at least twenty large pilchard cellars or 'palaces' for storing fish and salt, as well as numerous lofts for storing fishing nets and other equipment.[8]

The catch, 1926

The Fox family of Falmouth, who were Quakers and one of the main fish merchants in Cornwall, owned a seine and cellars in Mevagissey. Barclay Fox recorded an exceptional catch of pilchards in his diary 'when my gig and lame steed reached the noted town of Mevagissey' on 29 August 1839, painting a vivid picture of the excitement and chaos as the huge catch was landed and bulked up.

There appear to be from 4 to 5000 hogshead, enclosed and cellared. I waded my way to our cellar & found W. Roberts at the head of 50 or 60 women bulking the fish. The town was given up to confusion. Everybody beside himself & no such thing known for 20 years – such a catch taken so early. Scoured the town with Coward who congratulates every acquaintance he happens to

Bulking pilchards,
St Ives, 1871

meet . . . At 8 there came in a load of fish from the *Bee* [a seine],
concerted with our Mevagissey one, & about 9 came our turn to
discharge. Such a scene I never saw. We were obliged to keep
watch with lanterns all the way from the quay to the cellar to keep
off pilferers...The place was covered with men, women and children, & baskets, all come to buy, beg or steal, as way might open.
However, with close exertion we got off with comparatively small
plunder, and kept the women hard at it till 11 in the cellar.[9]

The next day he was up soon after five o'clock and spent the morning
supervising the sorting and packing of the fish. 'Before dinner I went
round nearly all the cellars in the place & made up the total amount to
be about 2874 hogsheads & as near as we can guess about 1200 now in
the seans [seines]. I left at 7 in a gig.'[9]

Reflecting upon the scene when he wrote his journal, Barclay Fox
wrote, 'This "town of stinks and wenches", as Coleridge says of Koln
[Cologne], – such muck, such hurry, such holla-ing, in cellar & out,
such universal pilfering whenever there is an opportunity. Such are the
sweet characteristics of Mevagissey in the fishing season.'[9]

# 3

# PHILIP WILLIAMS
# MARINER AND SMUGGLER

*The inhabitants had strong characteristics, and were known for their*
*pushing, restless, energetic life – priding themselves more on daring*
*deeds than on moneymaking. The sea was their workshop; and fishing,*
*fighting, privateering, smuggling and trading was their work.*

MATTHIAS DUNN, *Men of Mevagissey*[1]

S MUGGLING IN eighteenth-century England was widespread and highly profitable. The government, who were losing huge sums in uncollected duties, attempted to limit smuggling activity at sea through customs officers situated at strategic ports. As the century

William Daniell: Boats making harbour at Mevagissey, 1825

progressed the smugglers became ever bolder in their efforts to evade the revenue men and avoid paying the high duties on spirits and other luxury goods. In some areas, though rarely in Cornwall, armed skirmishes between customs officers and groups of as many as a hundred smugglers broke out. When he became Prime Minister in 1794 the younger Pitt's solution to the problem was to lower duty, first on tea, then on tobacco and spirits. This made smuggling less worthwhile and encouraged the increased purchase of drink, tea and tobacco so that the total duty collected by the government went up. At the same time, as we shall see, measures were introduced to make the capture of smugglers by the revenue more effective.

Nevertheless, in distant Cornwall, smuggling was still rampant in the late eighteenth century. It has been said that almost everyone in Mevagissey participated in the various smuggling enterprises that flourished in the town at this time.[2] Agents from France and the Channel Islands linked up with businessmen in towns such as Polperro and Mevagissey and these business associates employed mariners and ships to bring the goods across the Channel to the Cornish coast. There, the goods were transferred to small boats, manned by fishermen, and brought to the shore. Waiting on shore would be those who had volunteered to transport the goods to hiding places in coves, on farms and even in churches. Finally, the goods would be bought by merchants, shop keepers and local people. Matthias Dunn described how 'Cellars and private rooms were soon built in all manner of out-of-way places many of which are to be seen today...Besides being hiding places for smuggled goods, these places were also shelters from the press-gangs who in war times were continually hunting the fishing villages and hamlets of Cornwall: in almost every chimney, above the fireplace, there was room for a man to stand up.'[2]

The most important people in the Mevagissey smuggling enterprises were Thomas Shepheard, the ship-builder, and Captain James Dunn, a mariner turned ship-builder and businessman. Thomas Shepheard built 60 vessels, averaging around 74 tons, between 1786 and 1815.[3] These vessels, mainly sloops and luggers, were fast, manoeuvrable and economic. They could be conveniently beached to load and unload cargoes and were the principal craft used for smuggling. As long as Thomas Shepheard was working in Mevagissey it was the main ship-building town in the Fowey port registration area, which stretched from Polperro to Dodman Point. One reason that smugglers preferred Mevagissey to Fowey was that Fowey swarmed with naval men and Customs officers, whereas Mevagissey was hidden beyond Gribbin headland and less well guarded. In the period from 1786, when ship registration became mandatory, until 1815, a total of 441 vessels were registered in Fowey. As many as 47% of these were transferred from Fowey to other ports, such as Guernsey, and 18% were seized for smuggling and subsequently destroyed or sold.[4]

As the eighteenth century progressed the daring and ingenuity of the smugglers increased. In 1792 the notorious Carter family held 40 gallons of rum, 739 gallons of brandy, 2,778 gallons of gin at Prussia Cove in Cornwall, protected by eight six-pounder guns.[5] When a smuggling case came to court in Cornwall the accused were almost always acquitted; no jury and few magistrates were willing to punish friends or acquaintances for deeds which they themselves could not disapprove of and might even have participated in. As late as 1835, when smuggling was thought to be on the wane, five men from Polruan were charged with being among some 100 smugglers who had fought

A cutter. The ship used by H.M. Customs for law enforcement.

Gravestone of
Richard Gill,
Mevagissey
churchyard

preventive men. They were acquitted after the Crown jury decided that the sticks with which they were armed were not offensive weapons.[6]

Richard Gill of Mevagissey was one of many who died in this dangerous trade. He was a member of the crew of the *Reward*, one of the ships owned and managed by Captain James Dunn. He was only 22 when he received a wound while at sea on board the *Reward* on 6 September 1788. Although the wound could well have been received by a fall or knock and many seamen died in this way, it is much more likely that it was a gunshot wound inflicted by a revenue officer. He is commemorated by this verse on his gravestone in Mevagissey churchyard:

Though boisterous Winds and Rageing Waves
Have Toft me to and Fro
In fpite of all by Gods Decree
I anchor here below.
Although at anchor here I ride
With many of our Fleet
Yet once again I muft fet fail
Our Admiral Christ to meet.

Not everyone in Mevagissey wanted to face the risks and violence associated with smuggling. William and James Furse were involved in the smuggling trade at the end of the eighteenth century and they asked their younger brother, Thomas, to join them. Thomas decided that 'such business did not suit my mind; the risk and danger they ran, and the immoral life they in general led, was what I disliked,' and he turned down their invitation. It was not, he confessed, that he had any worries about smuggling being illegal or criminal. In the past he had helped to land smuggled goods and carry them into the country and had been well paid for the work. The truth was, he decided, he was not a man who enjoyed taking risks. Moreover, he was able to earn a reasonable living from his share in a seine and work as a cooper and shipwright.[7]

It seems that the 'immoral life' and risks involved in smuggling were no deterrent for Walter Williams' father, Philip, and his grandfather, Richard, who I discovered from the Fowey Custom House Ship Registers had both captained ships engaged in smuggling.[8] It was rather a shock to realise that I was descended from smugglers for, however acceptable the trade may have been in Mevagissey at the time, it was still a criminal activity. Smugglers described themselves as 'free traders' and claimed that they were helping others by selling goods at a cheaper price than the government would allow. There is no doubt that the high taxes imposed by the government on goods imported into the country caused great hardship to the working people of Cornwall as they struggled to earn a living from the sea or land. Salt, for example, which was required in large quantities to preserve the fish for export to the Mediterranean, was heavily taxed and therefore frequently brought from France by smugglers. More usual cargoes imported by the smugglers were, of course, brandy, rum, gin, tobacco, tea, lace and silk.

Lawrence Banks, an agent in St Austell for the Guernsey firm Carteret Priaulx, was a part owner of three Fowey sloops, *Brother*,

St Peter Port, Guernsey

*Saint Michael* and the *Eagle*. Richard Williams, of St Austell, was a close associate of Lawrence Banks and a part owner and sometime master of two of these ships. They were quite small vessels. The sloop *St Michael* was 37 foot long and 16 tons and had been built in Mevagissey by Thomas Shepheard and registered in October 1786. The *Eagle* was a 44 foot, 37 ton sloop, built in Cardigan but registered in Fowey in 1790. The men with the money held the power and Lawrence Banks, as a Guernsey agent, was an influential figure and one that the men who commanded the ships would want to have on their side. As the master of smuggling ships Richard Williams, Philip Williams' father and, it seems, my great-great-great-great-grandfather, was himself a vital link in the chain of people smuggling cargo from Guernsey to Cornwall.

In 1795 Thomas Shepheard built a 70 ton barge, named the *Charlestown* after the new harbour that Charles Rashleigh was constructing at West Polmear, near St Austell. Thomas Shepheard was named as her owner when she was registered on 4 March but in June he sold his shares to Joseph Dingle, merchant of St Austell and father-in-law of Richard Williams, who also acquired shares in her at this time. This barge was in service for 55 years, longer than any other Fowey-registered vessel. Philip Williams took over as the master of the *Charlestown* on 20 August 1798. He was then just 20 years old.[9]

*Left*: A smuggler
*Right*: A preventive officer. Drawings by William Heath, *c*.1830

Accounts for the ship-building business of James Dunn and Thomas Henna survive in the National Archives and show that Philip Williams was paid on several occasions between 1803 and 1806 for the transport of spars and pitch.[10] This appears to have been a perfectly legitimate business undertaking. However, at the same time Philip was involved with other ships whose activities were definitely illegal.

In 1803, for the first time, Philip Williams acquired shares in a ship. The *Fortune*, which had been built by John Willcock at Fowey in 1803, was an impressive 51 ton cutter with 10 ports. Ownership was shared between John Willcock and Philip Williams, who was also the master. The existence of the ports indicates that the ship was armed with guns. We do not know for sure whether Philip Williams was at the helm when the *Fortune* was seized for smuggling in 1806 and carried into Castlehaven in Ireland but it is more than likely. The Register was taken from the Captain and the owners found their investment worth nothing at all.[11]

James Dunn of Mevagissey, ship-owner, smuggler and ship-builder

If Philip Williams was the master of the *Fortune* on this unfortunate voyage, then it must have been a rather chastened man who eventually presented himself to his wife in Mevagissey. After the humiliation of losing not only the ship but also her precious cargo, he would have had to get home from Ireland by cadging lifts in ships or carts and by walking. In Philip Williams' house there were now three children. Philip had been baptised in 1798, Thomas in 1804 and Walter in 1807. Jenifer Williams must have been struggling to feed her children and to survive. In 1808 tragedy overtook the family. It seems that a virulent disease, possibly smallpox which was prevalent at the time, led to the deaths of the older Philip Williams on 19 October 1808, his mother Mary ten days later and his father Richard on 14 November.

It is said that in 1805 Captain James Dunn decided that smuggling could no longer be reconciled with his dedication to Methodism. More plausible reasons for his change of heart are the increasing success of the Revenue in combating smuggling and the reduction in duties on spirits, tobacco and tea. In 1805 two of Dunn's vessels, the *Lottery* and the *Venus*, were seized and in 1806 another of his ships, the *Heed*, was seized and broken up.[12] However, on one of his last smuggling trips to Roscoff in France, which had taken over from St Peter Port as the main smuggling port, he allegedly brought back a cargo on which he made a clear profit of £3,000. James Dunn had already invested some of his profits in his ship-building business and he now began to build, at great expense, a state-of-the-art privateer, the *Fame*. He also built himself a fine new house in Fore Street.

The Anti-Smuggling Act of 1805 acted as a powerful deterrent to smugglers. It made any vessel found within 100 miles of the coast with illegal goods on board liable to forfeiture. For the first time the anti-smuggling laws were extended to the Channel Islands, where it was forbidden to carry spirits, wine and tobacco to or from the islands in vessels of less than 100 tons. Naval officers, as well as Customs officers, were given the power to impress any detained smuggler. Some smugglers who might have endured a prison on land could not face the harsh conditions and discipline enforced upon a naval ship.[13] These measures certainly deterred some smugglers but others, tempted by the profits that could still be made, merely transferred their business from Guernsey to Roscoff and continued their risky trade.

# GROWING UP IN MEVAGISSEY

*Sir, if at any time you might be nigh unto Mevagissie, I shd. Esteem it a*
*great favour if you wd. come and preach to the people, for in this town,*
*there is much licence and drunkenness. The souls of the people cry out for*
*a lead away from their sin, but the church gives it not to them. There-*
*fore, like sheep without a shepherd, they stray from the true ways of*
*godliness, and are in great need of Salvation.*

MARY LELEAN TO JOHN WESLEY, 1753[1]

W ALTER WILLIAMS, the son and grandson of sailors and
smugglers, was born on 2 August 1806 and baptised on 7
January 1807. He grew up in the close-knit, rough-and-ready
atmosphere of early nineteenth-century Mevagissey with his two
brothers, Philip, who was six years older, and Thomas, who was just
two years his senior. Philip and Walter, following family tradition,
spent their working lives at sea; Thomas became a butcher. If I am
right in deducing that the Philip Williams who died in 1808 and was
buried in St Austell church was their father, then their mother Jenifer
will have brought the boys up on her own. Frustratingly, after discover-
ing the date of Walter Williams' birth and baptism, I was unable to find
one shred of evidence of his activities, or even existence, for the next
twenty-two years of his life. I had to build up a picture of life in
Mevagissey in these years from the information I could glean from
books, local collections, contemporary documents and newspapers.

The people of Mevagissey worked together, lived in close proximity
to each other and invariably married each other. Family and family
relations influenced business and daily life in every way. The closeness
of the large families is emphasised by the well-established custom of
giving children the wife's maiden name as a second name. Walter's
mother had been born Jenifer Langford and following tradition he was
christened Walter Langford Williams. The most populous family in

37

Mevagissey at the time of the 1851 Census was the Dunn family, nearly all of whom were connected to the sea and working as fishermen, sailors or ship-builders. In fact, there were ninety-four people called Dunn in Mevagissey then and between fifty and sixty Furses, Barons and Hunkins. Fishing boats and sailing ships were often manned by members of one extended family from 70-year-old grandfathers to 13-year-old boys. When a family member was sick or died, relatives would help out, often welcoming orphaned children into their already over-large families. In business, too, these close links were vital; they could ease or impede the flow of custom, credit, know-how and almost everything affecting the difference between profit and loss. Although the community might appear close-knit and inward looking, because of the sea it was also outward looking and enterprising; to go to sea at all was a risky endeavour. Men from Mevagissey did not only fish or smuggle for a living; many of them earned their livings working on the ships which travelled around the coast, or around the world, collecting and delivering goods. These ships, or vessels as they were invariably known, were the short- and long-distance lorries of their time. To sail by sea delivering goods may sound a more romantic occupation than to drive a lorry, but the reality of life at sea was tough, unpredictable and dangerous.

The brigantine *L'Oiseau* was a prize captured from the French by the Royal Navy in 1800 and brought into Plymouth harbour. She was acquired by a group of mariners and merchants from Mevagissey, renamed the *Seven Brothers* after the seven sons of William Lelean (who had drowned in September 1801), and registered in Fowey on 29 December 1801. The managing owner, John Pearce, who described himself as a gentleman, was a merchant from Mevagissey who owned and managed fishing seines and coastal and foreign-going ships and, probably, smuggling ventures. As well as the Dunn family, the Lelean family was pre-eminent in every aspect of sea-faring life in Mevagissey at this time. Some of the success of these two families must have been due to the large number of sons they had who were able to carry on their fathers' businesses and start new ones. Both families were active and fervent Methodists, even though John Wesley was known to disapprove of smuggling. William and Nicholas Lelean (the oldest of the seven brothers) and James Dunn all held an interest in the *Seven Brothers*. For these men the purchase of the 116 ton *L'Oiseau* was an

*Opposite*: Mevagissey toshers and luggers, 1910 (H. Hughes)

Nicholas Lelean

exciting business venture, but also an uncertain and speculative one. The repairs required before she went to sea were carried out in the Lelean or Dunn yard and in the summer of 1805 Nicholas Lelean sailed from Mevagissey in her, having said his farewells to his wife Catherine and their six small children. The mate was James Dunn, the 17-year-old son of James Dunn. The *Seven Brothers* had hardly left the bay when a French privateer bore down on her. The French boarded the ship and in the ensuing struggle two of the crew were killed and the rest captured and taken to Brest. From Brest they were marched to prison at Arras.[2]

Nicholas Lelean's letters from prison in France, to his wife and the managing owner of the *Seven Brothers*, John Pearce, make poignant reading. Occasionally 'prisoner Lelean', as he sometimes called himself, received a letter from his wife. Catherine told him in a letter of 8 October 1809, that although care and anxiety had clouded her mind she was endeavouring to live a life devoted to God. She gave him news of their children. Nicholas, now fourteen, had been working in a seine. She received 4 shillings a week for his labour but it had been such a poor year for pilchards that he received nothing for the fish. She told her husband that she would follow his wish and have Nicholas apprenticed to a shipwright. Thomas, who was twelve, worked with his uncle John for Mr Shepheard, the ship-builder. The oldest of their children, Ann, worked in Mr John Pearce's fish cellar. Catherine, clearly a strong and resourceful woman, taught the youngest children herself and opened a small Dame school in order to earn some money for the family. Both Nicholas and Catherine's letters are filled with lengthy protestations of their love of God and their confidence that He will care for them and give them the strength to cope with their troubles.[3]

Captain Lelean was eventually released in 1814. He had been in

France for nearly nine years. When he arrived back home a great crowd, accompanied by the town band, processed to the top of the hill in Mevagissey to welcome him. The Williams family, with young Walter now aged 7, must have been part of the crowd for this momentous homecoming. Catherine Lelean could not face the ordeal of joining the crowd to meet her husband; she waited for him at home. Their youngest child, Catherine, eight weeks old when he went away and now nearly nine years of age, was sent to meet him. He was greatly moved, as were the assembled crowd. In the harbour below the *Seven Brothers* lay at anchor, captured once again from the French.[4]

The Williams family, like the Dunns and Leleans, were staunch Methodists and the boys will certainly have attended the Methodist Sunday school where reading and writing were taught as well as good behaviour and religious observance. Walter wrote a good hand and he may well have attended a school in Mevagissey. It might have been a Dame school, like that run by Catherine Lelean when her husband was imprisoned in France, or it could have been one run by a retired mariner who would have taught the boys mathematics and rudimentary navigation. The art and science of sailing and seafaring was passed from father to son and, as Walter's father had died, other male relatives and friends will have shown him the ropes. Walter will have learnt to row and sail and fish as a boy and followed his older brother, Philip, around the quays and on board his ships when they came into Mevagissey harbour. As a young lad Walter may, like the Lelean children, have worked in a seine, in a fish cellar or at one of the local ship-building firms. The normal route to joining the merchant navy was to become an apprentice on board ship. Apprentices were expected to work hard for seven years for almost no money. The agreement drawn up on 1 January 1810, when Nicholas Lelean the younger was apprenticed to James Dunn in the ship-building business, is uncompromising. Nicholas would be looked after by James Dunn and 'instructed in the art of SHIPWRIGHT' and, in return, he was expected to carry out his master's lawful commands gladly, not commit fornication, or marry, play unlawful games, haunt Taverns or Playhouses or absent himself from his Master's service.[5] Many apprentices found themselves exploited and treated little better than slaves; Cornish papers of the period often carried notices from masters appealing for the return of apprentices who had run away.

When John Wesley came to Mevagissey he is said to have preached in fisherman Jimmy Dunn's loft; a large, long area with wooden beams and a wooden floor. On 13 September 1768 Wesley wrote in his journal: 'I preached in the evening at Mevagissey. It was a season of solemn joy I have not often found the like. Surely God's thoughts are not as our thoughts: Can any good be done at Mevagissey?'[6] Perhaps he was referring to the split he perceived between the growing number of people in the town who professed to be Methodists and their continued drinking and involvement in the smuggling trade, both of which he condemned. By 1785 the loft was felt to be too small and James Dunn was appointed to approach the Duke of Buckingham to obtain a piece of land on which to build a chapel. The Duke was not helpful and it was twenty years before the first chapel was built in Bank Terrace in 1805. By then, of course, in theory at least, Captain Dunn had given up smuggling.

The claims made for Methodism's success in reforming the population of Cornwall and other areas, such as Wales, where it was widely followed, are extravagant but there is no doubt that it had a tremendous impact. In 1851 the government conducted a census on religion and worship. All those who attended church or chapel on a certain day were registered. In Cornwall only 27% attended an Anglican church whilst 60% attended a Methodist chapel. One of Captain Dunn's sons, Samuel, became a well-known Methodist preacher. He claimed that in Cornwall,

> Tens of thousands of its inhabitants have been turned from darkness to light. From the power of Satan unto God. It has taught them to renounce the sins and recreations of smuggling, sabbath-breaking, cock-fighting, bull-baiting, hurling and wrestling: and has converted them into a Sunday-keeping, chapel-going, hymn-singing, prayer-offering, intelligent, moral, and religious people.[7]

Samuel does not mention the demon drink, perhaps the only solace left after all those other pleasures had been removed, but of course temperance and teetotalism were also vigorously promoted by the Methodists, particularly amongst sailors.

There was one popular aspect of Methodism that added colour and

entertainment in place of all the enjoyable, but now proscribed, recreations. As the Cornish historian, A. K. Hamilton Jenkins, has written:

John Wesley,
by L. Freeman

> Revivals formerly did much to enliven the tedium of everyday
> life in remote villages. The sight of the converts jumping over
> their seats and singing and shouting at the top of their voices in
> their new-found joy provided rich food for gossip if it did nothing else. Even the scoffer found pleasure in the spectacle of one
> of his neighbours crying unto the Lord to 'curtail the works of
> the devil', whilst another 'brother' was beseeching the Almighty
> 'to cut his tail right off'.[8]

Many of those so dramatically converted forgot their vows once the
excitement had died down, only to feel the call and get converted all
over again at the next revival. But many others tried hard to emulate
the example of Wesley and lived lives of patient endurance and self-
sacrifice.

Samuel Dunn had been converted to Methodism at St Austell in the

Philip Ball's house and bank in Church Street, Mevagissey

great revival of 1814. He established Sunday Schools in St Austell, Mevagissey and Gorran before volunteering to go to the Shetland Islands where there was an urgent need for preachers.[9] Samuel Dunn's biographer, the Mevagissey writer and journalist T.R. Harris, dubbed him the 'Apostle of the Shetlands' because he managed to increase the number of Methodists there from 235 in 1824, two years after he arrived, to 1,200 in 1828. Later, he became notorious for his disagreement with, and subsequent expulsion from, the Methodist Conference. There is a window in Truro Cathedral commemorating the Wesleys. It is dedicated 'To the Glory of God and in memory of Captn. James Dunn, a friend of John Wesley, and of his sons, Edmund and Samuel, formerly of Mevagissey.'

Life was hard in Mevagissey, and in the rest of the country, in the years following the end of the Napoleonic wars. In 1815 there had been approximately 100,000 men in the Royal Navy; in 1816 there were only 35,000. As well as the desperate shortage of jobs there were widespread shortages of food. In Cornwall, where farmers had previously provided enough grain for the population, there were shortages of corn not only in the populous mining areas, but also in agricultural areas. On 7 July 1815 the Italian market was reopened and efforts were made in Mevagissey to revive the fishing industry and valuable export trade, on which so many lives depended. Local merchants Philip Ball, Peter Smith, John Pearce and others helped to finance the fitting out of the fishing boats and by 1816 there were 30 seines in the harbour licensed and ready to go to sea.

Philip Ball had founded the Mevagissey Bank, which issued its own notes, in 1807. He was one of the first men to have extensive interests in the exploitation of china clay, which was to become one of the main exports from Cornwall in the nineteenth century. He also had shares in tin and copper mines, including the famous Polgooth tin mine on the outskirts of St Austell. He was a co-lessee of Mevagissey Harbour and Charlestown Harbour, a founder partner of the St Austell foundry and a partner in the St Austell Bank, Ball, Hamilton & Co., which operated from 1819 to 1822.[10] His bank and home were in Church Street,

44

Mevagissey, but, like any aspiring gentleman, he also bought land and owned farms. However, Philip Ball over-stretched himself and on 25 November 1824 his banking company, Philip Ball & Son, suspended payments. The bank's collapse was followed by the failure of other local businesses and many people in Mevagissey faced hardship and poverty as a result. Philip Ball had been a leading member and supporter of the Independent, or Congregationalist, church and at first it seemed that this might have to close.[11] The close family and business ties of this church meant that they suffered the most; the Methodists were less affected. In the following year, 1825, many other 'country' banks were to fail following excessive speculation, particularly in South American shares. Over 100 of about 700 such banks were forced to close and only 20 of these reopened. In 1826 new legislation lifted restrictions on the size of partnerships and introduced the principle of joint stock banking.

There was considerable unrest, nationally and locally, over the Corn Laws. They had been introduced by the government in 1815 to protect agricultural interest, by imposing duty on imported corn. Only when the price was very high (80s. a quarter) was the duty dropped. Fears that the export of corn from Cornwall to other areas of the country would lead to local shortages or price rises led to a disturbance in Mevagissey in November 1825 when women and boys gathered at the harbour to express their displeasure at men loading wheat for shipment to an eastern port. The local newspaper reported that 'The persons employed in conveying the wheat, became irritated and resorted to blows, which were returned by the sturdy dealers in fish,

Mevagissey Bank one pound note, 1821

with which the place abounds, and the husbands, brothers, etc. of the Amazons coming to their assistance, a general scuffle ensued, which ended in the ripping up of a number of the sacks, and the scattering of wheat which they were unwilling their fellow countrymen should eat, about the streets.'[12]

National and local events such as the war with France, the lack of work at the end of the war, the shortages of even basic food such as corn and the collapse of Philip Ball's bank, inevitably affected the lives of the people of Mevagissey. Life was not easy for those who had to care for their extended families whilst coping with the possibility of unemployment, bankruptcy, hunger, sickness and the early death of the main breadwinner in the mines or at sea. It is hardly surprising that people flocked to the chapels of the Nonconformists to be reassured of a better life in the hereafter if they lived sober and moral lives according to Christ's teaching.

# 5

## MASTER MARINER

*No man will be a sailor who has contrivance enough to get himself into a jail; for being in a ship is being in jail, with the chance of being drowned...A man in jail has more room, more food, and commonly better company.*

SAMUEL JOHNSON

I N THE NINETEENTH century Mevagissey was part of the port of Fowey, as it is today. As I began to explain towards the end of Chapter 1, there are two main sources of information for ships of the period: the local Customs House Ship Registers and the Registrar General's Seamen's Agreements and Crew Lists. The Fowey Ship Registers, which contain information on the type of ship, its size, its shareholders, each shareholder's occupation and the ship's demise, are held at the Cornwall County Record Office. The Agreements and Crew Lists, which describe the voyages and crews of ships, are at the

The Schooner *Snowflake* at the Quay, Mevagissey

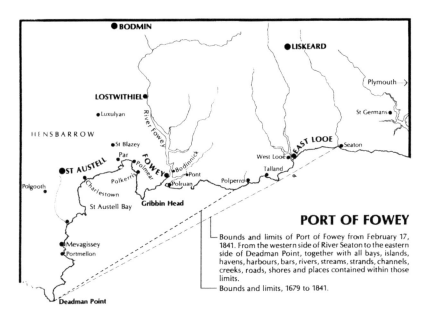

PORT OF FOWEY

Bounds and limits of Port of Fowey from February 17, 1841. From the western side of River Seaton to the eastern side of Deadman Point, together with all bays, islands, havens, harbours, bars, rivers, streams, strands, channels, creeks, roads, shores and places contained within those limits.

Bounds and limits, 1679 to 1841.

The port of Fowey. 1679–1841, Dodman Point (Deadman) to Polperro. 1841 to the present, Dodman Point to Seaton

National Archives at Kew. There are, however, many other records. Late in my research I received by post from the National Maritime Museum in Greenwich the Claim for a Master's Certificate which Walter Williams had applied for in March, 1851. This was a stroke of luck because, whereas previously I could only guess at the life Walter Williams had led before he became the master of *Brilliant*, the Claim listed all the ships that he had served on before the date of his application.[1]

Walter Williams first went to sea as an Ordinary Seaman in September 1828, when he was 22, on board the *Susanna* of Fowey. From April to September 1829 he served as a Seaman aboard the *Churchill*, a Truro ship in charge of his older brother Philip. Ship-owners were often reluctant to risk sailing in the winter and the document showed that Walter was not at sea at all during the winters of 1828–30 or for the period December 1830 to March 1832. When he went to sea again, in March 1832, it was as the master of the *Susanna*.

At the National Archives at Kew I ordered and received a large box containing the first surviving Seamen Agreements and Crew Lists for Fowey-registered ships. Carefully placing the papers in the box lid I was despairing of finding anything to do with Walter Williams when, mixed in amongst the ships starting with the letter 'S', I found his name as the master of the *Susanna*. Here was the very piece of paper that my great-great-grandfather had sent to the Customs in December 1835. The document was turning brown and flaking at the edges, but

48

remained complete and legible. It revealed that all the crew, except for the mate, William George, who was from Milford in Wales, were Mevagissey men; William Dunn, aged 22, N. Butland, 60, and F. Robins, 16. The paper also showed that in the six month period, starting 1 July 1835, the *Susanna* had sailed to Llanelly, Mount's Bay, Neath, Fowey, Swansea, Charlestown and Bristol.[2]

The *Susanna* of Fowey first appears in the Fowey Ship Registers on 29 April 1830. She was a 58 foot, 82 ton, counter-sterned schooner with a female figurehead and had been built at Plymouth in 1801. In 1830 James Dunn owned forty-eight shares in the *Susanna* and the master mariner, John Furse, sixteen. In order to finance the cost of building a ship and spread the risk several people usually owned shares in ships. From 1824 each ship had 64 shares and all owners and changes of ownership had to be entered in the Registers. Shareholders were usually either relatives of the main owner or tradesmen involved in the building and fitting out of the ship: rope and sail makers, blacksmiths and block-makers, merchants and innkeepers. But the owners often also managed to persuade other local people such as butchers, builders, grocers, quarry owners, school masters, farmers, lawyers, surgeons and even clergymen, widows and maiden ladies to make an investment in their ship. In the port of Fowey, owners tended to be about one-third mariners, one-third others whose income was derived from the sea and one-third land-based investors.[3] Ship-owning was invariably a community enterprise with most of the investors in locally-built ships coming from Mevagissey, Fowey, St Austell and the surrounding villages. There were occasionally investors from Truro, Falmouth, London or further afield. On 14 March 1835 James Dunn put the *Susanna* up for sale by auction at the Ship Inn and her new owner and master was 29-year-old Walter Williams. He owned twenty shares, his friend Samuel Allen owned eight and his brother, Thomas, who was a butcher in St Austell, owned four.[4]

I was surprised to see that the occupation of Walter Williams listed in the Ship Registers was Joiner and not, as one would expect, Mariner. A joiner, according to the dictionary, is someone who makes furniture, house fittings and other woodwork that is lighter than a carpenter's work. However, joiners were also employed by shipwrights. In his accounts for building the *Gallant* in 1839 the Polruan shipwright Nicholas Butson listed the men who constructed the hull as shipwrights, joiners, caulkers and sawyers.[5]. If Walter started his apprenticeship as a joiner when he was 14, as was customary, then he would have begun the seven years in 1820 and completed them in 1827. Presumably, he then worked as a joiner for a year before his first voyage aboard the *Susanna* in September 1828. At this time the main owner of the *Susanna* was James Dunn. Stitching together the various pieces of evidence it is difficult not to speculate that perhaps Walter Williams did his apprenticeship in the ship-yard of James Dunn and that during the winters of 1828 to 1830 and the period December 30 to March 1832, when he was not at sea, he was again working in the Dunn ship-yard. Perhaps it was James Dunn who encouraged him to go to sea in the first place.

There are not many accounts of life on a merchant sailing ship from those who actually sailed in them in the nineteenth century. The most famous is by an educated American, Richard Dana, whose vivid account of his *Two Years Before the Mast* has become a classic. At the time of his voyage in 1834 he was studying law at Harvard and undertook the voyage mainly in the hope that a change from studying would result in an improvement to his eyesight. He was also motivated by a spirit of adventure and love of the sea, but the romance did not last long. As a result of the appalling conditions and brutality he witnessed on his two-year voyage from Boston around Cape Horn to the west coast of California and back, he devoted the rest of his life to working to improve the conditions of seamen's lives aboard ship.

There is another account which, because it is much closer to the experience of Walter Williams and the other mariners of Mevagissey, seems more relevant. *A Victorian Sailor's Diary* was written by Richard Behenna of Veryan, which is just down the coast from Mevagissey, in 1888, some years after the events he describes had taken place. He recounts how in 1854 he joined the *Pheasant* of Fowey at Plymouth and made several voyages taking china clay from Par to Glasgow, Dort in Holland and North Shields. At Shields, which is on the north bank of the River Tyne about 8 miles to the east of Newcastle upon Tyne, the crew loaded, probably with coal, for Charlestown. On the voyage down they sailed into a storm: 'The wind died away for a short time, then it rose again to a heavy gale, blowing the canvas to rags. . . The sea took the jiboom [jib boom] away and two jibs with it. We lost bulwarks on the fore part of the ship with the same sea that the boom and jibs went…We got to a place called Dungeness. Many of the fleet suffered worse than we did. There was near 100 vessels in company with we.'[6] As well as coping with the vagaries of the wind and sea, Behenna had to put up with drunk and violent crew members. Like Dana he describes the arguments and fights on board which often resulted in the sailors being beaten and locked up in irons. There were other deprivations and difficulties. On a voyage from Alexandria in Egypt, provisions aboard were running low and the crew were cut to one biscuit and half a pint of water a day. At night 'the rats were bad on us; they would get in our beds, and eat our toe nails right down to the flesh, and sometimes, they would draw blood from us.' After nine days on these debilitating rations they finally arrived at Queenstown in Ireland. 'We was a nice looking lot when we got to Queenstown,' Behenna wrote, 'half starved and no water to wash our skin for the last two weeks.'[7]

The main reason that a sailor put up with the appalling conditions on board ship, enduring months on end in cramped, damp, filthy, rat-infested quarters with rough and often violent companions and appalling food, was, of course, economic. A sailor went to sea because he needed to earn a living and however risky and unpleasant the conditions on board a sailing ship, it was the life he was used to. As we have seen, there was not a wide choice of occupation for men in places like Mevagissey. Once a man became a master, life at sea became very different. The master sailed in the same ship all the time and often came to regard it as a second home; he was no longer subject to the arbitrary discipline of unpredictable masters and mates; he had a far greater say in where he went and what his ship carried and, above all, he had the opportunity to earn considerably more money.

The increase in his earnings enabled Walter Williams, at the age of 31, to think of marriage. The girl he chose, Ann Allen, was a Mevagissey girl and a member of the large Allen clan, many of whom were seafarers. The couple were married in Mevagissey church on 17 May 1837. Ann's parents, Anthony and Elizabeth, had each been married before and their family links are both immensely complicated and, as so often in the little Mevagissey community, immensely important. Anthony had retired from the sea to help Elizabeth run the King's Arms on the Jetty, which had previously been managed by her father. Their first child, Ann, who was to become Walter Williams' wife, was

born on 8 January 1809 and they had three more daughters, Louisa, Elizabeth and Sophia, the last-named born in 1815 when her mother was forty. The girls had six half-sisters and brothers from their parents' previous marriages. One of Elizabeth's children, Mary Penhall, had married Walter Dunn, a son of the famous mariner, smuggler and ship-builder, James Dunn. Walter Dunn was to become a close friend and business associate of Walter Williams.

A month after the marriage of Walter and Ann momentous events took place in London. King William IV died and eighteen-year-old Queen Victoria succeeded to the throne. The colourful period of the Regency had been followed by a period of reform under William IV, when slavery was abolished and the Reform Bill had at last made its way onto the Statute book. The young Queen now began her long reign, an era of innovation but with much emphasis on family values and duty.

After the death of Anthony Allen in 1812, aged 48, his wife, Elizabeth, continued to manage the inn herself, presumably helped by her daughters. Perhaps this business was a victim of the failure of the Mevagissey Bank because it was put up for sale on 8 April 1826. The advertisement noted that it was of modern build and in excellent repair and comprised a good kitchen with a vault under the bar, two parlours, a large dining room, eight lodging rooms, a cellar, a brewhouse, a stable and a wash kitchen. Property at this time was often leased on one or two or more 'lives'. In this case the inn was sold for 'the remainder of the term of 99 years, determinable on the deaths of two healthy lives, aged respectively 38 and 54 years'.[8] In August 1858 the King's Arms was damaged by fire and later reopened in Fore Street.

Walter and Ann Williams set up their first home in Cliff Street where most of their neighbours were fishermen. At the time of the 1841 Census on one side of their house were the families of John Dunn and Edward Dunn, both fishermen and with one son working as a fisherman. The mason Matthew Over lived on the other side and next to him Ann's mother, Elizabeth, now aged 65 and of 'independent means'. On 25 February 1838 Ann Williams had given birth to her first child, a girl, Jane Allen Williams. She was named, according to local tradition, Jane after Walter's mother with the second name Allen, Ann's maiden name. She was baptised a month later on 21 March 1838 at the Mevagissey Wesleyan Chapel where she was the first baby to

*Opposite:* Life on deck was much the same in the 1870s, when steam tugs first came to Fowey, as in this photograph from the 1930s

Cliff Street,
Mevagissey

have her name officially registered. As an adult she became the devout and strict Granny Pearce mentioned in the Introduction. I once asked my mother if her grandmother had been a very religious person. 'She thought she was,' she said. Soon after his daughter's birth Walter Williams left the *Susanna*. The Fowey Register of Ships indicates that in July 1838, Henry Furse took over as her master. On the 8th March 1839 Walter Williams sold eight of his twenty shares to Samuel Allen; it seems that he was anxious to devote his time and energy to a new project.

# 6

# THE BRILLIANT

*Build me straight, O worthy Master!*
*Staunch and strong, a goodly vessel.*

LONGFELLOW

WALTER WILLIAMS had sold his shares in the *Susanna* because he wanted to build his own ship. Although ship-building was a flourishing business in Mevagissey the establishment of new yards was hampered by the lack of available space in the town. The Lelean ship-yard was situated on the east side of the harbour close to the present Museum; this had probably previously been the site of the Shepheard yard where so many sloops and cutters had been built in the heyday of the smuggling trade. In the early twentieth century, when Percy Mitchell was apprenticed in the Roberts yard at the lower end of Chapel Street, new boats were pulled by hand on low-wheeled trolleys through the narrow streets to be launched from the quay.[1] It is not surprising that over the years the Dunns, the Roberts and the Mitchells chose to construct their vessels at nearby Portmellon where there was considerably more space. Launching, however, was a problem here too.

In 1839 Captain James Dunn was 85 years old and he had passed the everyday operation of his ship-building business to his third and oldest living son, Walter. In the tithe map of 1840 Walter Dunn is shown as the owner of a small part of the Penwarne estate at Portmellon comprising a moor, a garden and a yard for which he had to pay the vicar an annual tithe of three shillings and ten pence. Presumably this had been passed on to him by his father, James, who still held a small area of garden nearby for which he paid the vicar eight pence annually.[2] The requirements for a ship-yard were modest; indeed, some ships were constructed in the open on beaches. At Portmellon there was probably a mould loft with space for storing timber below it, another

Portmellon *c.*1884. The Anchorage is on the far right and at the top of the map opposite. © The Francis Frith Collection.

wooden building for storage, a saw pit and enough space outside for the construction of a ship. Walter Dunn, a relation by marriage and close friend of the Williams family, was the man Walter Williams had invited to help him realise his dream of sailing in a ship that had been specially designed to incorporate those features which, experience had led him to believe, were required in a ship trading in the Mediterranean. His ship would need to be strongly constructed but with lines that would enhance the vessel's speed; the hold would need to be commodious to accommodate large and varied cargoes but also allow the ship to sail well without ballast; the sail plan would need to be designed to enable the vessel to sail as fast and as safely as possible. Portmellon was where it would be built.

Walter Williams and Walter Dunn chose to build a schooner. The schooner had been developed in the Napoleonic Wars and the War of 1812 against America when it was found that, when sailing to windward, it was able to outdistance its much larger square-rigged pursuers.[3] A schooner had 2 or 3 masts with fore and aft sails. Above the gaff sails were set square or triangular gaff-topsails. By the mid-nineteenth century the schooner had replaced sloops and cutters to become the most favoured vessel in the merchant sailing fleet in

Britain. Walter Williams and Walter Dunn designed a ship of about 80 tons: large enough to undertake long foreign voyages and small enough to get into Mevagissey harbour. The two men would have discussed the kind of timber they would need and where they might find it. Although there were occasionally advertisements in the local paper at this time for sales of oak and other wood, most trees in Cornwall had long ago been axed for use as charcoal for tin smelting or timber by the navy.

The first stage in building a ship in the larger ship-yards at this time was usually to construct a scale half-model about three or four foot long, a representation of one side of the proposed vessel. Drawings were rarely made. The model would be shown to the owner and modifications made. The shipwright and owner would adjust the contours to fit their requirements for speed or seaworthiness. The designs of Mevagissey-built ships were traditional. They had evolved through trial and error and, as we have seen, at the end of the eighteenth century they were sought after for their speed, handling qualities and reliability. It is possible that the two Walters did not even make, or have made, a half-model. Small ship-yards often relied on eye alone.[4]

Walter would have been familiar with each step of the evolution of the ship as the shipwrights built the keel and the skeleton of the hull began to take on the recognisable shape of a merchant vessel. As a

Map of Portmellon, O.S. 1885

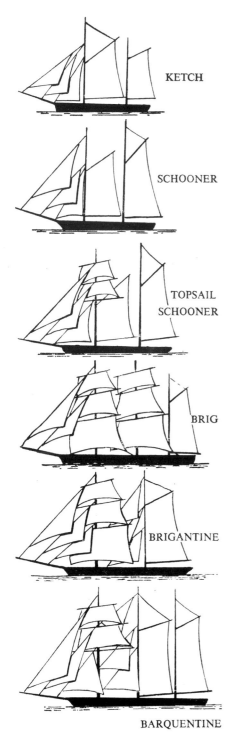

KETCH

SCHOONER

TOPSAIL
SCHOONER

BRIG

BRIGANTINE

BARQUENTINE

joiner he would probably have worked on the hull and been able to monitor progress closely, making suggestions and planning the next stage. Masters and owners took pride in their vessels and, as this was his first ship, he would have been especially attentive to detail. He would have asked a shipwright who was skilled with a chisel and enjoyed fancywork to carve the figurehead, which was the typical half-length female form, well draped, and may have represented his wife, Ann. Perhaps he made it himself. Some figureheads were crudely made but many were skilful examples of folk art.

To build a ship was a considerable capital investment and, of course, a very risky one. For an ambitious young man like Walter Williams it was a logical step towards greater control over a vessel and her operation. Sailing a small schooner around the coast of Britain or across the Mediterranean or Atlantic was a highly skilled undertaking. Everything depended upon the master. He needed to be a competent seaman and have sound knowledge of navigation, weather and tides. He was often the only man on board who could navigate with skill enough to enable the ship to arrive at the right place and negotiate the often hazardous entrances to ports and harbours. He had to get to where he was expected to collect a cargo at the right time and then drive himself and his crew to sail speedily so that his freight could be delivered on time. He was in competition with other captains and owners and the amount of work that came his way would depend on his reputation as an efficient and reliable operator. I have been told by one of his great-grandchildren that Walter Williams had a reputation for being always the first into port and that the *Brilliant* was known as a fast schooner.

There is not very much at the National Archives in London about Mevagissey so it was exciting to find the papers of Dunn and Henna, ship-builders,

amongst the plans for the building of the harbour of 1776 and quibbles about tithes with the Rector of Mevagissey. The account books for Dunn & Henna, from 1799 to 1806, list the payments for every item or service they bought for every ship they built or repaired.[5] All Mevagissey at the turn of the century seem to be in the Dunn & Henna accounts. Amongst the suppliers are Peter Smith, sailmaker, William Pearce, ropemaker, John Libby, blacksmith and Nick Allen, cooper. Among the workers are the familiar surnames of Jago, Hugo, Lelean, Furse, Scantlebury, Brokensha, Jolly and Ball. Goods arrive for Dunn & Henna from Fowey, Falmouth, Lostwithiel, Cardiff, Truro, Plymouth, Bristol and London. The largest expense in any ship was the timber: deal, oak and elm. There were snatch blocks for about two shillings each and single blocks for about one shilling each. A gaff, a squirrel boom and a ring tail boom cost nine pounds. When writing about ships, then as now, one has to learn a whole new vocabulary – topsail yard, mizzen mast, mizzen yard, jenny yard – as well as words that have almost disappeared from our vocabulary such as tallow, rosin, verdigris, junk for wads and faggots of furze. The ship-yard ordered hooks and thimbles, brooms and baskets, lead, copper, nails,

The three-masted schooner *Mary Barrow* unloading coal at North Quay, Falmouth

*Opposite*: Types of sailing vessels

59

Half-model of a ship in Mevagissey Museum

paint, oil and tar. When James Dunn went to Fowey, Falmouth or Truro on business he usually hired a horse and charged expenses for overnight stays. When he went to Plymouth and back by coach it cost him two pounds. Shipwrights were paid between 1s. 6d. and 3s. 10d. a day. Sawyers, who worked in pairs, were together paid 3s. a day, and foremen between 3s. and 5s. The costs soon mounted and the total cost for the *Fame* cutter, which was fitted as a privateer with guns and cabins, came to £1,874, which is a rate of seven pounds and seven shillings a ton for the 136 ton ship.[6] A more usual cost per ton at this time was about five pounds. On that reckoning Walter Williams' ship would have cost him and his shareholders about £500.

The time taken to build a ship varied enormously, from six months to a year or more. As Walter Williams appears to have been a man in a hurry, his ship probably took about six to nine months and would therefore have been started in the summer of 1838, perhaps soon after Walter had handed the *Susanna* over to Henry Furse in July. Although Walter would have been anxious to get his ship into the sea in order to earn some return on his investment, he would also have been careful to make sure that it was seaworthy and safe. Merchants were unwilling to trust their goods to a ship unless it had been inspected and an inspection was also necessary if the ship was to be insured. Walter Williams asked William Broad, the Lloyd's Inspector from Falmouth, to come and see the ship when she was still on the stocks and 'nearly planked up'. The planks, which had been steamed to make them pliable, were fixed onto the frame with iron or copper bolts. Mr Broad came on 2 March 1839 and his detailed report survives in the National Maritime Museum. The ship was just over 60 feet long and 17 feet broad and her hold was 10 feet deep. Everything was made of English oak except for the 'plank from the keel to the first foothook heads which was composed of English elm', a wood better able to withstand immersion in sea water. The masts, yards, sails and rigging were all new as were the windlass and rudder. The ship was provided with 6 anchors with the appropriate amount of chain, towlines and warp. There was a long boat for conveying the crew to shore and for use as a rescue boat. The inspector returned for a second inspection and reported that 'she is well built and the whole of her materials are of good quality and she should in my opinion stand 11 years.' On 26 March 1839 she was given the top grade of A 1 for 11 years.

At Portmellon ships were launched down a slip at high tide. Sometimes new ships were launched before the fitting out had been completed and this was then done in a dry dock but as there was no dry dock at Portmellon or Mevagissey Walter's ship was probably almost finished when she was launched. As master, Walter would have chosen the type of sails, the rigging, the cordage, and arranged the fitting out of the forecastle for the crew and his own cabin at the stern. Then at last the ship was ready for launching. This was a great moment for the owners and the ship-yard. Sometimes there were bands and flags and the event was often reported in the local newspaper. For example on 8 March 1833 the *West Briton* newspaper reported that the schooner *James Dunn* 'glided from the stocks in fine

Mitchell's boatyard, Portmellon. Drawing by F. Hilden-Percy

The schooner *Louise* on the stocks ready for launching at Gannel Yard, Newquay, 1877

style amid the cheers of about 200 spectators'. Often the wife of the owner, or some other important person, was called upon to break a bottle on the ship's bows as she slid into the water.

Walter Williams called his ship the *Brilliant*, a popular name for ships at the time. Walter owned ten of the sixty-four shares and sixteen other people, an unusually large number of shareholders (although the maximum number permitted was 32), owned the rest. Ship-owning at this time was a community venture and all the shareholders were likely to be relatives, friends or acquaintances of the main owner. One can imagine Walter rushing around, standing drinks to people and cajoling them into investing in his new venture. Samuel Allen, then a grocer but later to call himself a ship-owner, and John Furse, a mariner, held four shares. They had both been shareholders in the *Susanna* with Walter Williams and he will have known them well. The only relatives to take shares were Walter Dunn, whose yard had built the ship, his brother Edmund Dunn, a London silk merchant, and Walter Williams' mother, Jane (Jenifer), who was then running a grocery shop. Two of the craftsmen who had contributed items to the ship's construction, John Pearce, ropemaker, of Mevagissey, and James Thomas, ironmonger, of St Austell, bought four shares. Four yeomen (landowners) – John Dingle, James Hill, William Northcott and Richard Julyan from Mevagissey, Gorran and St Ewe – were shareholders as well as the miller, James Profit, from Caerhays.* The other shareholders were Thomas Kitchens, a merchant, and two spinster sisters, Emma and Henrietta Gummoe, from St Austell.[7] In the evening after the launch of the *Brilliant* shareholders, relatives and people who had contributed to the construction of the ship would have congregated in one of the public houses, perhaps Walter's mother-in-law's old inn, the King's Arms, or the Ship, to celebrate the great occasion.

* I have been told that Walter Williams was related to the Williams family of Caerhays House. The support Walter Williams received from neighbouring landowners and the miller from Caerhays may indicate that this is true. I have found no other evidence to support the claim.

# 7

# A WATERY GRAVE

*Low in the caverns of the deep*
*Beside some coral, dead he lies*
*Wrapped in seaweeds there to sleep*
*Till from the grave of death*
*He rise, yes, he who came to tell and save*
*Shall raise him from this watery grave.*

*William Dyer, who was unfortunately drowned off*
*Holyhead November 28, 1849, at the age of 18 years.*

GRAVESTONE IN MEVAGISSEY CHURCHYARD

I HAVE INHERITED an octant; that this curious instrument was a vital navigational aid seems extraordinary. It is made of wood and brass with small mirrors and is both functional and elegant with floral decoration on the brass and a calibration made of ivory or bone. It must have belonged to Walter Williams and, as it was made in the mid-eighteenth century, was perhaps inherited by him from his father. At the

Royal Observatory at Greenwich, where they have many examples of the quadrant, the sextant and the octant, I struggled to understand how the instrument worked. Basically, it was a reflecting navigational instrument used for measuring the altitude of heavenly bodies and thus calculating a ship's position. Octants remained in use by navigators until the nineteenth century although the sextant, which was introduced in the mid-eighteenth

*Opposite*: The *Elwood* of St Ives

*Left*: The octant I have inherited

65

century and used to measure the altitude of the sun at noon, became the most usual instrument in calculation of longitude. Some of the instruments at the Royal Observatory were engraved with the name of a naval ship or a captain or a maker but sadly mine has nothing on it to suggest to whom it might have belonged or who might have made it.

I like to think that as Walter Williams prepared for the first voyage of the *Brilliant*, hiring his crew, ordering the food for the voyage and assembling the cargo, he may have taken this very octant to his cabin. The ship would still have smelt of the ship-yard, of sawn wood, linseed oil and tar, as he brought aboard his sea chest, his compass, his charts, nautical books and oil lamps. The seaman's chest was made of wood and then tarred to keep it dry, and sometimes decorated. In it a seaman would keep all his clothes. He probably also had a ditty box to keep his valuables and personal items such as letters from home. The master's cabin was a triangular space built into the stern of the ship. The two long sides of the triangle were lined with narrow seats backed by panelling rising about three feet above the deck. Above this was a shelf with a low rim to prevent objects falling from it. Over this, panelled lockers sloped back to the deck head. Between the seats was a small table. There was usually a fire. The master would spread out his charts on the table and study them by the light of his swinging oil lamp.[1]

On the 18th March, 1839 the five members of the crew joined their captain on board the *Brilliant* for her maiden voyage. They were all Mevagissey men except for a young seaman from Bude called Thomas Pascoe, who, with Henry Tregilgas, had previously sailed with Walter Williams aboard the *Susanna*. As his mate he had a very experienced sailor, Anthony Martin Rollings, the middle one of three generations of Mevagissey seamen with the same name. This Anthony Martin had been the master and an owner of the *John* and was now 40 years old. Like Walter he had married a member of the Allen family, Jane, and according to maritime records he was tall for Cornish men of that period, five foot eight with dark brown hair, a sallow complexion and hazel eyes with a mole on one eyelid. Also on board were Nicholas Collier, who was 21, and his brother, Richard, who was the ship's boy and only 13 years old.[2]

The crew's quarters were in the forecastle. They were simply furnished with a table and bench seats and frame bunks or hammocks, which could be folded back against the wall. Below the benches was storage for oilskins. Here the crew ate and slept. The mate might have a separate cabin in the forward part of the ship or near the captain's cabin. The first month's wages were paid in advance to the crew so that they could buy gear and clothing. The crew often felt, therefore, that they worked the first month for nothing or, as they put it, were 'flogging a dead horse'. A canvas horse stuffed with wood shavings was hoisted up and dropped into the sea at the end of the first month on some ships. The crew also had to supply their hammocks or mattresses, which were filled with straw and known as a donkey's breakfast. Folding bunks came into general use in the mid-nineteenth century; before that apprentices were sent to the sail yard to buy canvas and then had to sew their own hammocks. They also had to supply bedding, towels, a plate, mug, knife and fork. The crew wore flannel shirts, a blue jersey or guernsey, heavy cloth trousers and a cap. A man's clothes were very valuable to him and carefully guarded because to replace them was expensive. When a man died his clothes would be auctioned off and the proceeds sent to his widow, if there were one, or given to the rest of the crew.

Details from a later, 1847, voyage of the *Brilliant* show that Walter Williams was paid £5 a month, the three seamen £2 and the apprentice fifteen shillings. The crew's allowance of food was as follows:

> One pound of beef or pork a day per man.
> One pound of bread a day per man.
> A quarter of an ounce of tea and of coffee per day per man.
> One gallon of water per day per man.
> One pound of sugar per week per man.

In handwriting the Articles specified that 'no spirits allowed but at such times as the master sees proper.'[3] Sailors were keen on, and expected, a certain amount of 'grog' (diluted spirits) but excessive drinking was a great problem with sailors, often as much amongst the masters and mates as amongst the ordinary seamen.

The *Brilliant* left Mevagissey on her maiden voyage on the 19th March 1839. This first voyage was similar to the coastal trips that Walter had been making in the *Susanna*; she went first to Liverpool, probably with china clay from Charlestown, then to London with

Sea boots from
Mevagissey
Museum

general goods, then back to Charlestown to load up with china clay for Gloucester. On the 2 July the ship was back in Mevagissey for a quick visit before setting off again for Liverpool and Gloucester and back to Charlestown on 3 September.[2] The next day Walter set sail for France with a completely new crew except for Thomas Pascoe. Richard Gill, a Mevagissey man, was the new mate and the rest of the crew came from St Ives, Bude and Charlestown. Their destination was Croisic and their mission to collect a cargo of salt for the pilchard industry. As we have seen, large quantities of salt were required in order to preserve the pilchards so that they could be consumed throughout the winter, and French salt was considered to be much better for this purpose than English salt. On 26 September they were back in Fowey unloading the salt.[4]

After a short break at home Walter began to collect his crew for the *Brilliant*'s first voyage to the Mediterranean. He must have been a courageous and adventurous man because as a sailor he had, until now, sailed only around the coast of Britain. Perhaps he relied on the knowledge of his mate, William Dunn, aged 54, a very experienced local seaman. Richard Gill, also a local man, was the second mate. The other members of the crew were Nicholas Jolly, a Mevagissey man, Mathew Langdon of Veryan, who had sailed to Croisic with the *Brilliant* and was now acting as cook, and Thomas Pascoe of Bude who had been with Walter Williams since 18 March. All the crew was on board in Mevagissey harbour by the 8 October. They then spent two weeks getting the ship prepared for the long voyage. The *Brilliant* eventually cast off and left for Naples on the 23 October 1839.[5]

One week later, as the *Brilliant* sailed down the coast of Spain, tragedy struck. Thomas Pascoe, the young man from Bude, was drowned.[5] Accidents at sea were not infrequent, especially in rough weather; the whole heavy, wooden machinery of the ship was dangerous. Booms and rigging might suddenly slam across the decks knocking down anyone in their way, men might slip if the decks were oily, and boys often fell from the high rigging as they attempted to reef

CREW DURING ABSENCE FROM UNITED KINGDOM.
SCHEDULE (C.)

Ship *Brilliant* of the Port of *Fowey* whereof *Walter Williams* was Master.

A LIST of the CREW, (including the Master and Apprentices,) at the period of her Sailing from the Port of *Fowey* in the United Kingdom, from which she took her first Departure, on her Voyage to *Naples* on 23rd day of *October* 1839 and of the Men who joined the Ship subsequent to such Departure, and until her Return to the Port of *Glasgow* being her Port of destination, in the United Kingdom, on 15th day of *February* 1840

| Name. | Age. | Place of Birth. | Quality. | Ship in which he last served. | Date of joining the Ship. | Place where. | Time of Death or Leaving the Ship. | Place where. | How Disposed of. |
|---|---|---|---|---|---|---|---|---|---|
| Walter Williams | 33 | Mevagissey | Master | Susannah | 16 Mar 1839 | Mevagissey | 15th Febry | Glasgow | Still on board |
| William Dunn | 54 | Do | Mate | Do | 7 Octr | Do | " | " | Do |
| Richd Gill | 35 | Do | 2nd Do | Roseland | " " | Do | " | " | Do |
| Nicholas Jolly | 21 | Do | Seaman | Helligan | 8 " " | Do | " | " | Do |
| Thos Pascoe | 26 | Bude | Do | Susannah | 2 " " | Do | 30th Octr | at Sea | Drowned |
| Matthew Langton | 24 | Vergan | Cook | | 7 " " | Do | 15 Febry | Glasgow | Still on board |
| Peter Rodgers | 22 | Montrose | Seaman | Henry Alex | 6 Decr " | Naples | " | " | Do |

*Thos Pascoe*

*Drowned*

NOTE.—If any one of the Crew has entered Her Majesty's Service, the Name of the Queen's Ship in which he entered must be stated in the Account, under the head of "How Disposed of."

Schedule C for the *Brilliant* 1839–40

in or adjust the sails in heavy weather. One can only guess at poor Thomas Pascoe's fate and hope that once he fell into the sea, his end was swift. Anyone wearing boots like the huge, leather seaman's boots on display in the Mevagissey Museum could not have survived in the sea for very long. Many mariners refused to learn to swim so that if they fell overboard they would not suffer a protracted struggle in the freezing water. A swift watery death was preferable to a lingering, losing contest with the pounding waves.

The Bay of Naples

# CORNOVAGLIA – NAPOLI

*The great bulk of this fish was landed at Naples; and it was a general custom with the ships' masters to engage a local artist to paint their vessels' 'portraits' whilst they were in harbour there. Forty years or so ago it was common to see in homes of seafaring families at St Ives and other Cornish ports watercolours of trim little brigs and brigantines painted perhaps a century before, with Vesuvius – the burning mountain – flaring in the background. These pictures have become very rare now; but where they survive, provide an interesting reminder of this old commercial link between Cornwall and Italy.*

CYRIL NOALL, *Cornish Seines and Seiners*[1]

T HE BRILLIANT tied up in Naples harbour to disgorge her cargo on 16 November 1839, having taken just 23 days to sail there from Mevagissey.[2] The ship and her crew would have been met by a jostling crowd of Italians hoping to persuade them to use their services or buy their goods. Amongst the confusion of porters unloading, traders selling liquor and supplies, were the notorious crimps who, acting as agents in procuring sailors for ships, endeavoured to tempt the sailors to part with their money in the bars and brothels of sailor town. Also plying for trade were pier artists hoping to persuade the ship's captain to have a painting made of his ship. Michele Funno accosted the Captain of the *Brilliant* with examples of his previous work and Walter, proud of his new ship, was rather taken with the idea of having a painting of her to take home to show his wife. The artist probably had the background with the volcano erupting and the fishermen in the foreground already painted by one of his assistants; he only had to observe the *Brilliant* with sails unfurled and carefully reproduce what he saw before him. The rigging had to be accurate or else the captain would complain. So he carefully painted the lines of the hull, noting the parallel white lines, blocked with black, to look as if the ship were carrying guns and thus frighten off marauders. He was used to painting ships and could accurately reproduce the sails, the ropes, the flags and other nautical details. The medium he used was gouache, which is an opaque watercolour. When applied on paper the effect is similar to that of an oil painting but it dries to a much lighter colour than it seems when wet. Although Michele Funno's representation of the ship is quite accurate, features such as the men on board and the bow waves look wooden and unconvincing. In spite of this, the mixture of sophistication and naivety work together to create an arresting image. Life on the high seas, the picture tells us, is exciting and rewarding and the places one visits are magical.

The merchant shipping trade had evolved in Mevagissey and other places in Cornwall, to transport goods to and from the area. Tin, copper, stone and fish were exported and coal and goods for the home brought in. For many years pilchards and other fish had been the main export from Mevagissey. The pilchards were caught by the seine fishermen from July to September and transported to Italy in the autumn. Each hogshead of pilchards was branded or stencilled on its top with the name of the curer, the year, name and place where cured, and name of its port of destination. Some of the ships continued to sail throughout the winter to get the fish to ports such as Ancona, Naples, Leghorn, Genoa, Venice, Civitavecchia and Trieste in time for Lent. Leghorn (Livorno) was one of the most important ports for the export of pilchards from Cornwall as the fish were carried on from there to nearby Pisa and Florence. It is interesting that I have only found one voyage made by Walter Williams where pilchards were his main cargo. In October 1844 at Mevagissey quay he loaded up with 149 hogsheads of fish, on which a harbour charge of 6d. a hogshead was charged and 53 hogsheads of fish for which 3d. was levied; the total charge was £4 8s. 0d.[3] Harbour and pilot charges, and charges for other items such as labour for loading and unloading, were a significant drain on a merchant ship's profits. He then went to St Ives, where he took on more pilchards, and from there he sailed to Naples. As the nineteenth century progressed, it became rare for Mevagissey ships to sail from Cornwall with pilchards. Increasingly, they sailed to the Mediterranean, America, Canada and the West Indies from the expanding ports of Liverpool, London, Glasgow and Bristol where they were able to find freights more easily.

In the eighteenth and nineteenth centuries enterprising British merchants had established businesses in ports around the world. Benjamin Ingham, for example, went to Sicily from Yorkshire in 1806 to sell the cloth produced in his family's firm. He quickly realised the potential of the local marsala trade and in 1812 constructed a huge fortified enclosure (known as a *baglio*) for his new business in Marsala. Ingham, helped by a ready supply of nephews, built up a huge business exporting wine to Britain and America. In America he invested in property (including in what is now 5th Avenue), canals and railroads. In Sicily he became one of the main exporters not only of marsala wine but also of sulphur, citrus fruit, olive oil, sumac (used in tanning), barilla (an alkali), almonds, filberts, pumice, brimstone, currants and even rags. He built his own fleet, including a steamship, lived with an aristocratic Sicilian lady and, in spite of sporadic revolutions, recurrent and devastating outbreaks of cholera and threats from the Mafia, built up an incredible fortune.[4] Walter Williams is unlikely to have exported Ingham's goods, as he had his own ships, but there was a large community of British merchants in Palermo and Messina requiring transport for their goods to Britain and the *Brilliant* often called at Sicily.

The *Superb* of Poole. This painting is remarkably similar to Michele Funno's of the *Brilliant* but must have been by an imitator as the quality of the work is inferior.

The port of Livorno

On mainland Italy Walter Williams called frequently at Genoa, Venice and Leghorn (Livorno) but the port he visited more than any other in Italy was Naples. I doubt that he spent much time admiring the scenery or exchanging more than a few cursory words with the Italians. He probably knew little or nothing about the complicated power struggles between the various regions of Italy, unless they impinged on his dealings with the local agents or the price of his freights. Naples at this time was part of the Kingdom of the Two Sicilies (Naples and Sicily) and ruled with cruelty and inefficiency by Ferdinand II, a member of the Spanish Bourbon family who had gained control of Naples in 1734. Britain was sympathetic to those who sought to overthrow Ferdinand and unite Italy, which did not happen until the 1860s.

Throughout the 1840s the British Consul was involved in negotiations to reduce the duty charged on goods brought to Naples from Britain. King Ferdinand had indicated that he wished to adopt a more liberal commercial policy to help reduce smuggling, which was widespread as ships attempted to avoid the heavy duty. British colonial produce was particularly highly taxed, with a 120% duty on sugar and 50–100% on coffee. Cod from Newfoundland was taxed at 37% and pilchards from Cornwall at 27%. The Consul, Sir Woodbine Parish, wrote to London that the Italians were more likely to reduce the duty on goods they did not produce themselves: 'Linens rather than cottons – twist perhaps and Colonial produce; especially the fish of Newfoundland which with British Pilchards and Herrings once

74

formed one of the most important branches of our trade with the Sicilies, now entirely destroyed by the excessive duties.'[5] The Treaty was eventually agreed and signed by Queen Victoria and King Ferdinand on 29 April 1845. No duties were to be imposed in either country based on tonnage, harbour use, lighthouses, pilotage, quarantine or other similar activities. The duties on cotton yarns was reduced by one-third, on cotton cloths by half and on silk goods by one-third; all this pleased the Lancashire merchants who had been pressing the government to help their export trade. But the most important change for Britain was the halving of the duty on fish from Newfoundland and Cornwall and goods from the colonies such as sugar and coffee.

The surviving records for ships sailing around the coast or to the deep waters of the Mediterranean and beyond enable researchers to build up an almost complete timetable of their voyages. We have seen that the *Brilliant* arrived at Naples on her first foreign voyage on 16 November 1839. After unloading she proceeded to another port in Ferdinand's Kingdom of the Two Sicilies, Palermo. The freight charges earned on a ship's outward voyage were often used to procure a cargo home. However, if the ship's agent in the port and the master failed to find a return cargo, the master might sail on to another port with a local cargo, or in ballast, in the hope that he would find a return cargo there. There were often long delays in port while the crew waited for a suitable freight to be found. On this occasion it was 2 January before the *Brilliant* left Sicily for Glasgow. On board was Colin Rodgers from Montrose, whom Walter had managed to recruit in Naples to take the place of poor Thomas Pascoe and who was no doubt happy to be getting a paid ride home to Scotland. The longer journey home, from Palermo to Glasgow, took over six weeks; twice as long as the outward voyage.[6]

Walter Williams had started his career as an owner of a merchant ship at the right time, for the trade was at its peak in 1840. He carried on sailing backwards and forwards two or three or more times to the Mediterranean every year, as far as we know without serious problems, for the next eight years. Unlike some owners and masters, who laid their ships up in the winter, Walter Williams kept sailing throughout the year. In 1841 he sailed to Naples, Leghorn and Palermo and back to London, Liverpool, Falmouth, Fowey and Mevagissey. He arrived at Liverpool on 27 December and commenced off-loading the cargo of

The schooner
*Lelean*, 1840

wine, olive oil, oranges, corkwood, brandy and retail goods. Some of these goods were delivered to Falmouth and the rest, 30 baskets of figs and 4 pots of honey, were a late Christmas present for himself and his family.[7]

The experiences of Richard Dana and Richard Behenna related in Chapter 5, and the tragic death of Thomas Pascoe on Walter Williams' first foreign voyage in the *Brilliant*, made me realise that Samuel Johnson was probably right when he claimed that 'being in a ship is being in jail, with the chance of being drowned.' The calm blue sea, the effortless progress of the ship, the friendly fishermen and the enchanting landscape shown in Michele Funno's picture of the *Brilliant* hid a very different reality for the merchant sailor. Seas were rarely so blue or so calm. The ship's progress was only made possible by the sailors working all hours in all weathers, living in appalling damp and cramped quarters on maggot-ridden and unhealthy food. The charming waving fishermen in the foreground of the painting might well be brigands and the romantic-looking port of Naples, seen in the background, could also be viewed as a dangerous place seething with drunken sailors, prostitutes, disease and secret cabals plotting to over-

76

throw the King. The sea itself was constantly buffeting and battering these ships, an ever-present threat to the unwary or simply the unlucky. The small wages the seamen and their master earned ploughing backwards and forwards on that long and hazardous journey from Cornovaglia, as the Italians called Cornwall, to Naples, were hard-earned.

Young woman knitting, Polperro

# HOME AND AWAY

*Heave away ye sons-of-thunder,*
*For the nor'ard we will steer,*
*Where the gals and wives are waiting*
*Standin' there upon the pier.*

*Cheer up, Jack, bright smiles await you*
*From the fairest of the fair.*
*There are loving hearts to greet you*
*And kind welcomes everywhere.*

*An' the gal you love most dearly*
*She's been constant, firm and true,*
*She will clasp you to her bosom,*
*Saying, Jack, 'I still love you.'*

SEA SHANTY 'ROLLIN' HOME'

L ONG ABSENCES had to be borne with patience and hope by the wives, mothers and children of mariners. The sad moment when the sailor left home shores and said farewell to his loved ones and the happy moment when the sailor returned and his wife or sweetheart clasped him in her arms were represented in countless contemporary paintings, prints, sea shanties and ballads. The sailor was leaving the feminine world of the home to join the masculine world of life at sea and yet he was, at the same time, going to another kind of home and another kind of woman. All ships were, of course, referred to as 'she', and often named after a wife or mother. A woman's bust, scantily but discreetly clad and carved from wood, would often grace the bows of the ship as her figurehead. In sailors' slang women were equated with parts of the ship; a woman's bustle was referred to as her 'stern' and her bust as her 'bows'. In sea shanties women are celebrated as virtuous and faithful wives but also as bawdy, flirtatious temptresses;

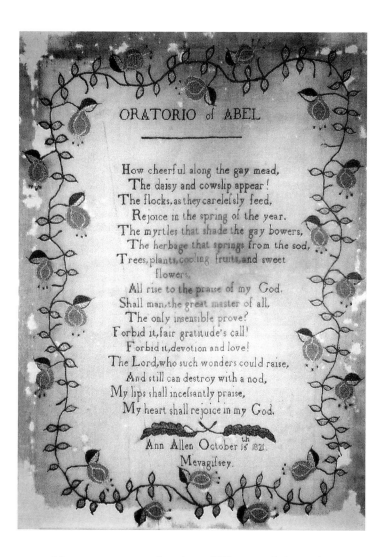

ORATORIO of ABEL

How cheerful along the gay mead,
The daisy and cowslip appear!
The flocks, as they carelessly feed,
Rejoice in the spring of the year.
The myrtles that shade the gay bowers,
The herbage that springs from the sod,
Trees, plants, cooling fruits, and sweet
flowers,
All rise to the praise of my God.
Shall man, the great master of all,
The only insensible prove?
Forbid it, fair gratitude's call!
Forbid it, devotion and love!
The Lord, who such wonders could raise,
And still can destroy with a nod,
My lips shall incessantly praise,
My heart shall rejoice in my God.

Ann Allen October 15th 1821.
Mevagissey.

A sampler made by Ann Williams (neé Allen) in 1821 when she was 12

on some ships toasts were drunk to 'Wives and Sweethearts – May they never meet!' When a ship arrived in port her sailors were only too eager, after weeks cooped up in the forecastle, to spend their money in the port's taverns, grog shops, dance halls and brothels.

Sailors were said to have a wife, or at least a mistress, in every port. I have no idea whether Walter Williams succumbed to the temptations of sailor towns in the ports he visited but we do know that he spent much more time away at sea than he did at home in Mevagissey. Here is his schedule from September 1842 to March 1844 which indicates that he was at home for less than two of those seventeen months:

| | |
|---|---|
| 17 September 1842 | Sailed from Falmouth for Palermo |
| 31 January 1843 | Arrived Liverpool having been delayed in Gibraltar by the illness of one of his crew members who died in the civil hospital on 18 January |
| 31 January – 8 March 1843 | In England |
| 8 March 1843 | Sailed from Liverpool to Naples |
| 3 August 1843 | Arrived Liverpool from Palermo 3 August |
| 3–20 August 1843 | In England |
| 20 August 1843 | Sailed from Fowey for Alicante |
| 7 March 1844 | Arrived Newry from Alicante[1] |

Inevitably Walter was rarely at home for the important events involving his family. On 5 June 1843, during the period shown above, his third daughter, Anne, was born as he was sailing from Liverpool to Naples. He was not able to see his new daughter until early August. Ann will have been helped with her new baby and with the other two girls, Jane and Elizabeth, who were then aged five and two, by her mother and mother-in-law and other close family and friends.

That there was a close support network amongst the women of the extended family at this time is shown in a fascinating document which

Market Square, Mevagissey

I found on the Internet, posted by a family historian from New Zealand. In June 1843 Walter's mother Jenifer (or Jane) Williams was a beneficiary of an unusual will left by Elizabeth Hicks of Ventonwin in the Parish of St Stephens in Brannel. Elizabeth Hicks was a spinster and, having no children to spend her money on, she appears to have squirrelled away a considerable fortune. She left over forty bequests, many of them to women; something highly unusual at the time. The cash bequests varied from £1, for her gardener, to £50. Most of the bequests were to members of her extended family of Hicks and Langfords. Walter Langford Williams' mother's maiden name was Jenifer Langford and Jenifer's mother had been born Elizabeth Hicks; presumably the Elizabeth Hicks who left this generous and complicated will was a cousin or an aunt. To 'Jenifer Williams of Mevagissey, widow of Philip Williams, late of Mevagissey, Mariner' she bequeathed £15: the equivalent of about a quarter of a year's pay for a master mariner at that time.[2]

When Walter's mother died on 23 May 1846 Walter was in Liverpool, having arrived there the day before, and it is therefore possible that he managed to get home in time for the funeral. Jenifer Williams' will was a very much briefer affair than that of Elizabeth Hicks. She appointed her middle son, Thomas, a butcher in St Austell and unmarried, her executor and instructed that within six months of her death he should sell by public auction all her freehold property and goods and chattels and divide the proceeds between her three sons.[3] Two years later, on 30 January 1848, Walter's wife, Ann, gave birth to a son, another Walter. After three daughters, the family will have been overjoyed by the arrival of a boy. Walter senior, inevitably, was not there – he was in Leghorn. However, the money he was earning sailing to the Mediterranean, helped by the money his mother had left him, enabled the family to move into a new house in Fore Street and to employ a servant to help Ann with the children.

Ann Williams will have been only too aware of the many Mevagissey men who lost their lives at sea. Like all the wives of mariners and fishermen she could only hope and pray that Walter would return safely after each of his long voyages to the Mediterranean and other parts of Europe. She will have known the wives of the Lelean family who lost many of their men at sea. William, the father of the Nicholas Lelean who had languished in French prisons for nine years, had

The *Snowdrop* at
Naples, 1846

drowned on 27 September 1801. While he was in prison Nicholas was
distressed to hear that his eldest brother, also William, had drowned.
Nicholas himself, back from his ordeal in France, continued his life as
a master mariner without further mishap. He helped his son, Nicholas,
who had been apprenticed to the ship-builder James Dunn while his
father was in France, to set up his own business. The first ship off the
stocks in 1823 was the *Pembroke*, followed by the *Catherine*, named
after his mother, in 1827. The five-year gap between the two ships does
not indicate that the yard was inactive; the major part of a ship-yard's
business at this time was in maintaining and repairing ships. In 1833
the *Snowdrop* of 116 tons had been launched with customary ceremony
in the presence of her new master John Lelean. In 1861 John's second
son, Mathew, took over as master of the *Snowdrop*. The following story
of Mathew and his wife Maria, discovered on the Internet, illustrates
the conflicting loyalties of the men and the anxieties of the wives of
Mevagissey mariners:

Mathew loved his ship almost like a person, so much so that his wife Maria, who did not share the fascination the sea had for her husband's family, became rather jealous of the inveterate hold the sea had over him and begged him to give up his wandering life and stay at home. Every year there was some tragedy of the sea in Mevagissey and she feared that even the proud *Snowdrop* of Mevagissey would be doomed to suffer disaster one day. Mathew did eventually sell the *Snowdrop*, and waited at home until the opportunity came to make the purchase he wanted. One day, he had a generous offer from a large ship-building firm in Newcastle to take command of one of their ships. He was an impetuous man and was about to accept eagerly but his wife dissuaded him for she knew that, strong as was the love of the sea in the blood of the Leleans, their pride was even stronger. A Lelean could never be another man's servant. He must always be his own captain; he could never sail under the orders of another. Mathew was still at home thinking about the proposition when his old ship, the *Snowdrop*, sailed under her new owners and was wrecked. All on board were drowned. Mathew was thankful for his wife's premonition and warnings; he gave up sailing after that.[4]

Ann Williams may well have tried to persuade her husband to give up the sea after he narrowly missed losing his ship and his life on three occasions in 1847 and 1848. On 18 December 1847 the *Brilliant* managed to reach Fowey harbour, laden with pilchards from St Ives, with the cargo dangerously unbalanced. Part of the cargo had to be landed and repacked before they could proceed. Loading a ship evenly and safely was a vitally important part of the preparations for a long voyage as overloading, or not taking care to balance the ship, was a frequent cause of capsizing. This time they were lucky and on Christmas Eve the *Brilliant* was able to set sail from Falmouth for Leghorn.[5] The voyage to Leghorn on this occasion took just over a month and the *Brilliant* tied up in the harbour on 26 January 1848.

It was fortunate that Walter had sailed for Leghorn on this voyage and not to Messina or Palermo because on 12 January a violent revolution had broken out in Sicily. 1848 was a year of revolution all over Europe as people struggled to achieve more liberal government. Italy, as we have seen, was at this period divided into a number of separate

states governed by autocratic rulers who did not take kindly to demands for constitutions and parliaments. Sicily, part of the Kingdom of Two Sicilies ruled by Ferdinand II, was the first area to revolt, followed shortly by Naples where Ferdinand, alarmed by the violence, granted the revolutionaries a constitution in February. In Rome the Pope was forced to flee in November and early in 1849 the Grand Duke of Tuscany left Tuscany. But by the autumn of 1849 all the constitutional experiments had ended and many of those who had inspired them had been killed or sentenced to long prison sentences.

In view of the unstable situation in Italy it is not surprising that British merchants looked to other markets for trade. When the *Brilliant* left Liverpool on 15 August 1848 she set out in a completely new direction, sailing round Denmark and through the Danish Sound to the Baltic.[6] Walter Williams did not sail to the Mediterranean again until 1852.

For centuries dues had been levied by the Danish crown on all ships travelling through the Sound. Complaints were regularly made about the dues, which consisted of a fixed duty on all ships over 40 tons and a smaller duty on vessels of lesser tonnage, with duties levied on cargoes of specific goods at a rate of one per cent. Most of the complaints arose from the manner in which the tolls were collected; vessels were often detained at Elsinore for non-payment of the dues, and this

Par harbour

caused needless expense as they might be held for anything from one day to three months.

While he was in Denmark Walter acquired a beautiful souvenir to take home to his wife. It was a large porcelain punch bowl decorated with a lively painting of a two-masted British ship leaving Kronborg flanked by rowing boats and a paddle steamer. For years Nancy Williams Bannister, who inherited the bowl (as well as her great-grandfather's name), thought it was a representation of Walter Williams' ship, but sadly this is not the case. It seems that the Ship Clearance Company of Major Wright & Co. of Elsinore had these bowls made as gifts for foreigners, and particularly the English sea captains who were their main customers. Major Wright had come to Elsinore in the 1760s and the firm he started in 1778 was one of the best-known clearance firms there. There are similar bowls in the collection of the Danish Maritime Museum at Kronborg and at the National Maritime Museum at Greenwich.

From Kronborg the *Brilliant* proceeded to Pillau, a seaport and watering place which was an important port for the export of timber

86

and flax to Britain. It was then in Prussia but in 1946 it became part of Russia and was renamed Baltiysk. It is situated on the narrow spit of sand separating the Frisches lagoon from the Baltic. The *Brilliant* navigated the narrow channel up which ships had to travel to reach the port. Here, the cargo of timber would have been especially carefully loaded to avoid it sliding around and unbalancing the ship. New regulations prohibited the loading of timber on the deck as this practice was seen as a major cause of ships wrecking in high seas. The *Brilliant* took the cargo to London, reaching Gravesend on 27 October and probably then continuing up to the Baltic dock, the first of the new Surrey docks which had been opened in 1809, to unload her cargo. London was the world's largest port and throughout the nineteenth century a huge dock-building programme was undertaken to make the port more efficient and competitive.

On 13 November 1848 the *Brilliant* left London for Antwerp, where the crew took on a cargo of grain and sailed for Bristol. On the morning of 16 December, as the *Brilliant* was sailing close to the Cornish coast, a fierce gale blew up. According to the *Royal Cornwall Gazette*, soon after daybreak when the gale was at its height, a vessel was seen near Par apparently in imminent danger, 'everyone expected her to founder, as the sea at times completely buried her.' The master had tried to enter Fowey harbour but, unable to weather Gribbin Head, he headed for Par. 'This was a most anxious and fearful time,' the newspaper reported. 'The people belonging to the harbour soon assembled on the breakwater (although the sea was then making a complete breach over them) to signalise and render all the assistance they were able, as this was the last and only chance for saving the vessel from destruction. She accordingly bore away for the pier and in a few minutes was got inside the breakwater in perfect safety.'[7] Walter Williams and his crew were safe owing to the captain's quick thinking in a dangerous situation but also to the new twelve-thousand-foot breakwater and harbour built at Par by local industrialist Joseph Thomas Treffry of Place in Fowey. 'I feel indebted for the preservation of our lives and vessel, under Providence, to the breakwater of Par,' Walter Williams was quoted as saying, 'for had it not been for this noble little harbour of refuge, no doubt our lives and vessel would have been sacrificed.'[7] The newspaper claimed that this was the eighth vessel saved since the breakwater's completion in 1835. The next item in the newspaper concerned a ship that had not been so fortunate. The *James Wearne* of St Ives foundered off Porthleven and the wreck was washed ashore. The master's watch was found in the wreck but there was no sign of the crew of six men and a boy.

The crew of the *Brilliant* did all they could to save the cargo of grain and, after calling in at Mevagissey on 27 December, were able to proceed to Bristol, where they arrived on 8 January 1849. Walter's wife, who, like all mariners' wives, lived in hope that her husband would not join the many others in a watery grave, must have been relieved and overjoyed to see him after such a close encounter with death.

The rest of 1849 was an unsettled period for Walter Williams and his ship. The only surviving record is that in *Lloyd's Register*, where beside the usual entry for the *Brilliant* (name of ship, type of ship, master, where built, port belonging to, voyages in that year, when surveyed and class given by the surveyor), is a little extra information apparently printed on with a rubber stamp and saying 'Stranded Pillau'. The fact that there are no crew lists may be because, as the ship was stranded, the crew and master did not return in the normal way to a port in Britain and hand in the Articles. We do not know how badly the ship was damaged, or if indeed it was. We do not know whether the crew was dismissed, which seems possible, while the master stayed in Pillau to get her towed off the sandbank somehow. One thing we do know, however, is that according to all the official records Walter Langford Williams never again sailed in the *Brilliant*.

# A DEADLY FOE

*The sea brought wealth to some Cornishmen; it brought a livelihood to many more; but to a few it brought loss, disaster, and death. It was even more fickle and wayward than the mines in its favours and depredations, an untrustworthy friend and a deadly foe.*

JOHN ROWE, *Cornwall in the Age of the Industrial Revolution.*[1]

T HE MERCHANT sailing business was flourishing in Cornwall in the 1840s although there was a good deal of unemployment in the mines. Emigration from Cornwall had started in the 1830s and increased greatly in the 1860s when competition from abroad severely damaged the profitability of the copper and tin mining industries. In 1866 alone twenty mines closed and 5,000 miners emigrated. Business in the Fowey area, including ship freight, was saved from collapse by the development of the china clay industry and the new ports for its export established at Charlestown, Par, Pentewan and Fowey.

J. M. W. Turner: Boscastle harbour. Teams of men on the cliffs are hauling the vessel along the narrow and winding entrance to the harbour to safety.

The wreck of the
*Cuiet* at Porthleven,
1884

Shipwrecks were an ever-present reality for the people of Cornwall and the raw material of countless broadsheets, pamphlets and books for the rest of the population. They were a tragedy for the families of those who drowned and invariably a financial disaster for the owners of the ships; not all vessels were insured and their cargoes were rarely covered. In 1835 a Select Committee was appointed by the government to inquire into the loss of ships and lives throughout the British Isles. It found that loss of life was 763 persons in 1816 and an average of 894 per annum in the years 1833 to 1835. The main reasons for the losses, according to the Committee, were faulty design and defective construction of ships, inadequate equipment, imperfect states of repair, improper and excessive loading of cargoes, incompetent masters, drunkenness amongst officers and crews, marine insurance which inclined ship-owners to take less care in the construction and safety of ships, the lack of safe harbours and faulty charts. The Committee recommended that a Mercantile Marine Board be set up in London to superintend and regulate the Mercantile Marine of the United Kingdom. The measures that the Board was to carry out were immensely important. They covered every aspect of maritime endeavour including the building, surveying, equipping and loading of ships and the education, health and regulation of crews and officers. In addition, Courts of Inquiry were to be set up to examine the cause of shipwrecks, with power to suspend negligent officers.

Amongst other measures, such as the requirement for the Crew Lists and Agreements which have provided so much of the information I have gleaned about Walter Williams, the Merchant Shipping Act of 1835 required the registration of seamen in order to create a means of manning the Navy in time of war. This first attempt at registration drew up an index of seamen from the Crew Lists. This system proved cumbersome and inaccurate and in 1844 regulations were introduced to establish a system whereby each British seaman leaving the country had to have a Register ticket. The ticket gave the seaman's registration number, his full name, place and date of birth, place of residence, the date he first went to sea and a physical description. The ticket system was unpopular and was abolished in 1853. Indeed, so unpopular was it that some seamen, Walter Williams amongst them, never had a ticket.

In 1845 voluntary examinations for masters and mates were introduced. Masters had to be at least 21 years of age with not less than six years' service at sea, and mates 19 with at least four years' experience at sea. The examinees had to be able to write a legible hand and understand the first five rules of arithmetic. All classes were examined in seamanship, rigging vessels, cargo stowage, navigation and nautical astronomy. They had to be able to put their ship's position on the chart by calculating latitude and longitude, or by compass bearings of points on the land. They needed to understand the use of the quadrant or sextant, observe the sun's meridian altitude, to obtain the latitude from it and determine the tides by the age of the moon. Examiners were appointed to test masters and mates for the standard qualifications in seamanship and navigation and to award them licences. At first the examination was voluntary and only applied to foreign-going ships, but after 1850 it was compulsory for all foreign-going vessels and all home vessels carrying passengers.

Walter Williams' older brother, Philip, applied for a certificate as a Chief Mate as soon as the scheme commenced. Unlike his brother, Philip had a Register ticket. He had been given the number 155243 at

Liverpool on 6 March 1845. The record states that he was 46 years old, with brown hair and blue eyes, and was five foot five and a half inches in height: small by today's standards but quite normal in Cornwall at the time. Because Walter never obtained a ticket there is no physical description of him in the records. It is stretching guess-work too far to suggest that he might have had similar features to his brother but, then again, it is likely that he was a similar height, and blue eyes seem to run in the family. Philip's son, also Philip, who was ticketed as a fourteen-year-old apprentice at Liverpool in 1849, was blond and had blue eyes. In 1859 he obtained the qualification of Only Mate at Bristol and became a Master at Bristol in 1861.[2] Masters could obtain their certificate as a result of examination or by exemption due to long service. Walter seems to have been one of those masters who felt that the many years that they had spent at sea should be qualification enough and he did not gain his certificate until it became compulsory, and then by exemption due to long service. It may be significant that he chose to gain his qualification at Cork in 1851, which was said to be by far the easiest place to gain a certificate.

In 1849 Walter Williams had parted company with the *Brilliant*. It seems likely that the difficulties of trading with Italy, as revolution swept the country, had a disastrous effect on the profitability of the *Brilliant* and forced Walter Williams to sell his ship and find another. Samuel Allen, who had been a shareholder and manager of the *Brilliant*, asked Walter to take over as master of a new and much larger ship, the *Zuleika*. The *Zuleika* was a 'Plantation' ship; one of a number of ships built in Canada, where there were limitless supplies of timber and ships were therefore cheaper to build, and brought to England. Between 1841 and 1880 37 plantation ships were entered in the Fowey Registers.[3] The majority of these ships, including the *Zuleika*, were constructed in Prince Edward Island, often by shipwrights who had emigrated there from Devon and Cornwall. The *Zuleika* was a square-sterned carvel-built brigantine, with a standing bowsprit, of 178 tons. Her owner, Samuel Allen, was ambitious and like many Mevagissey men he had several different occupations – often at the same time. In 1839 he called himself a grocer, in 1841 he appears on the Census as a fish carrier and by the time the 1851 Census was taken he had become a ship-owner. He had bought the *Zuleika* from Henry Hazard of Charlottetown in Prince Edward Island and was the sole owner when she was registered at Fowey on 29 September 1848. On 1 August 1849 Walter Williams joined the *Zuleika* in Liverpool with a crew of ten men and boys. The responsibilities of managing a ship that was over twice the size of the *Brilliant* and with more men to supervise might have been found daunting, but Captain Williams was now 43 and, as a tough, seasoned Mevagissey mariner, he was probably quite ready for a challenge.

The *Zuleika* arrived at Swinemunde, a Baltic port in Germany, on 20 August 1849. She loaded with timber and left harbour for England, arriving in Harwich on 27 September and London two days later. She unloaded her cargo and proceeded, probably with a new cargo, to Cardiff. She left Cardiff on 26 November for Plymouth but shortly after leaving port the ship caught a bank and began to fill. The damage sustained was considerable and the cargo was discharged.[4] Once again, Walter Williams had to wait around and supervise the repairs on a ship that he had put aground. It is doubtful whether there was enough time for him to go home to see his fifth child and fourth daughter, Sophia Susan, who had been born while he was in the Baltic on 7 September 1849.

In his career to date it is unlikely that Walter Williams had ever sailed across the Atlantic. The records of his early career as a seaman show that he only sailed in the home trade around Britain and, from 1839, to Italy and other parts of Europe. He had already taken on the challenge of sailing a much larger ship and now, 2 March 1850, the *Zuleika* sailed from Cardiff for Wilmington in North Carolina. It is tempting to speculate that perhaps Sam Allen had bought the *Zuleika* in order to cash in on the demand from emigrants for passages to America. He was the Mevagissey agent for ships taking emigrants from Plymouth so will have been aware of the business potential in this trade. In Torquay, for example, the local timber merchant who owned ships for importing timber from Canada had built up a lucrative trade carrying emigrants on the outward voyage. [5]

Walter Williams must have had to buy new charts and study them carefully before he set out on this new voyage. The ship arrived in Wilmington on 1 May, having taken two months to cross the Atlantic. From Wilmington the *Zuleika* sailed on to Jamaica. She stayed in the West Indies all summer and did not set sail for home until August. Now laden with the typical colonial produce of coffee, beeswax, arrowroot, ginger, rum, logwood (used for dyeing black, blue and grey), fustic (yellow dye) and pimento she made good progress and arrived at Liverpool on 28 September.[6] The following year, 1851, Walter again set out to cross the Atlantic but this time to Rio de Janeiro in South America. He left on 21 April and did not arrive until 8 July. Once again he stayed in the area for several months and did not leave until 9 October. The voyage home took nearly 3 months and when he eventually arrived back in Gravesend on 24 December he had been away from home for eight months.

**FOR SALE,**

BY PUBLIC AUCTION, on WEDNESDAY the 9th of April, 1851, at Two o'clock in the Afternoon, at MALPAS, in the *Truro River*, the well known fast sailing SCHOONER

"B R I L L I A N T,"

THOMAS LEY, Master, per register 80 2997-3500 tons will carry 130 tons. Built at *Mevagissey* in March, 1839, well found in stores and may be sent to sea at a trifling outfit, will take the ground well, transport without ballast, and in all respects well adapted for the Foreign and Coasting trade.

For viewing the same, apply to the Shipkeeper on board; and for further information to Mr. SAMUEL ALLEN, of Mevagissey.

WILLIAM ROBERTS, Auctioneer.
Dated Mevagissey, 18th March, 1851.

Sale of the *Brilliant* advertised in the *West Briton*, 1851

Just before Walter left for Rio de Janeiro, on 28 March 1851, the advertisement reproduced above had appeared in the *West Briton*. The glorious *Brilliant*, so strikingly depicted by Michele Funno in Naples, was on a downward slope. Her speed, which had meant that Walter Williams could be first into port and cover the journey to the Mediterranean in record times, was no longer to be tested. She was bought by Mr James Mollard and re-registered at St Ives, where he lived, and put to work as a Coaster transporting natural materials from Cornwall to Wales and returning with coal. Many ships from the south and north of Cornwall were occupied in taking clay, tin, copper and stone from Cornwall to Gloucester, Runcorn and Liverpool and returning with coal from Wales for use in the clay and tin mining industries. This was an unglamorous life; it was as if a racehorse had been harnessed up to work as a carthorse. The *Brilliant*'s light dimmed and

her romance faded as she tramped around the coasts of Britain. On 17 November 1854, loaded with copper ore for Swansea, she was leaving Portreath on the north coast of Cornwall when disaster struck. She had got as far as the pier head with all her sails hoisted when, just as the quay warp was cast off, the wind dropped. The strong ebb tide and heavy ground swell caused her to drift onto some rocks and there she stuck. On the next high tide the local hobblers, who were employed on land to tow vessels by rope, managed to haul her up on the beach and the cargo and ship's materials were saved. However, on the next tide the *Brilliant* became a total wreck.[7] Her sails, masts and timbers were battered by the waves and thrown back upon the beach where a crowd waited to cart away anything of value. The large old timbers would be used in buildings, the smaller pieces saved and dried and then used on the fire. The famous wreckers of Cornwall, notorious in the old days for fighting over the spoils of wrecks and even taking rings from the fingers of dead sailors, found little of value as the crew had already saved the sextant, the compass, the lamps and their own chests. But who claimed the *Brilliant*'s female figurehead? Perhaps it was washed away at Portreath, like so many seamen, to a watery grave. At least, in this wreck, there was no loss of human life.

The entrance to Portreath harbour

In Fowey the average life for the ships on the register in 1850 was 39 years.[8] The smaller coastal vessels, the sloops and barges, appeared to have longer lives with the *Charlestown* barge, as we have seen, in service for 55 years. The *Brilliant* was only fifteen years old; she had been struck down in her prime. Walter Williams' earlier ship, the *Susanna*, had also been lost. When Walter Williams had left the *Susanna* in 1839 he had sold his shares to his closest friends and associates, Samuel Allen and Walter Dunn. Subsequently Walter Dunn became the main owner with 48 shares and he therefore bore the main financial loss when the *Susanna* was lost at sea on the first of January, in the fateful year of 1849; the year he himself died from cholera.

## KING CHOLERA

*Mevagissey is a town*
*A church without a steeple*
*A heap of dung at every door*
*And most unsociable people.*

DEATH WAS never very far away in Victorian England. In Cornwall accidents in the mines, deaths at sea, diseases such as typhoid, cholera, tuberculosis and smallpox, carried many people off to an early grave. Life expectancy in the mines and for mariners was about 40 to 45 years. For women and infants the hazards of child birth often led to an early death; a cursory look around any churchyard will soon reveal a child's grave. Following a death the body of the deceased would be washed and dressed and placed in an open coffin in the parlour of his or her home, so that people could visit and pay their last respects. In Mevagissey, relatives or friends of the dead person would then carry the coffin up the hill to the churchyard for burial. Those who could afford it marked the grave with a gravestone or monument, but poorer people were buried in unmarked graves, which after a few years might be dug up again.

On 10 July 1849 Mary Jane Kendall was buried in the graveyard of St Peter's Church, Mevagissey. She was seven years old and she had died from cholera. Two days later Jane Cloke Hedges, aged eight, was buried. She, too, had died from cholera. On 15 July the first adult victim, James Ball, who was 30, was buried. The sickness spread with alarming rapidity; just one month after the death of Mary Jane Kendall, ninety people had died in the little fishing town. When the cholera had run its course, in the autumn, 125 people had died from the population of around 2,000.

Cholera inspired fear and panic. No one knew where it was going to

97

strike next and who it might bear away. There seemed no logic or pattern to its spread. The symptoms were sudden and severe, distressing and disgusting. A person might rise in the morning feeling fit and well and be dead by the evening. Although children and old people in Mevagissey seemed, at the start, to be the most vulnerable, in the end no age group was safe from the terrible symptoms. One of the many unpleasant effects of the disease was to turn the victim's skin blue. The working classes called it 'King Cholera', because the 'blue' of the patients reminded them of the supposed 'blue blood' of royalty. There was little doubt that the poor were the most at risk and in Mevagissey this meant the fishermen and their families, living as they did in damp and overcrowded houses clustered around the harbour with, as the rhyme above says, 'a heap of dung at every door'. Household waste, animal and human excrement were left rotting and stinking in the yards outside the houses and fish guts and waste were piled outside the fish cellars around the harbour. The putrid smells arising from these heaps were breeding grounds for disease and an affront to visitors.

In the panic following the outbreak of cholera in Mevagissey between 600 and 800 people immediately left the town. Fishermen set out in their boats for neighbouring harbours such as Gorran, Charlestown and Par where they could carry on their work. The local undertaker was a victim of the disease, which meant that coffins had to be sent over from St Austell. The St Austell men refused to come into the village but left them at the top of the hill for collection. Bread, newspapers, the mail, food supplies and medicines were all delivered in the same way.[1]

Fear of the disease led some to behave uncharitably. On the morning of 11 August a fishing boat from Mevagissey, manned by Henry Johns and Daniel Oliver, arrived at Fowey. Dr Illingworth was called to see Daniel Oliver who was unwell and he prescribed medicines. By about two o'clock Oliver's condition had deteriorated and he showed definite signs of cholera. The doctor arranged for him to be placed on a fishing boat in a warm cabin with a quantity of straw and blankets and jars of hot water around him. He visited him four times and was with him when he died. But once Daniel Oliver's Mevagissey friends realised that he had cholera, not only did they refuse to go near him or help him in any way, they even refused to row the doctor out to the boat.[2]

A month later, on 21 September, a letter in the *West Briton* drew

*Opposite*: The river at Mevagissey in the 1920s

attention to another sad case and the unfortunate repercussions which resulted from it. Two sailors died aboard the *Chronometer* of Mevagissey (the last ship built by Walter Dunn, in 1842) while the ship was moored in Fowey. Local people refused to allow the bodies to be interred in the churchyard at Fowey or in the fields on either side of the river and the bodies were therefore taken out to sea and thrown overboard. The writer of the letter deplored this uncivilised behaviour which took no account of the relatives' grief. He also pointed out that throwing bodies infected with cholera in the sea had already prejudiced people against fish and harmed the fishing industry on which so many local people depended.

The health experts considered that the insanitary condition of the village and harbour were responsible for the rapid spread of the disease. The Mevagissey doctor, Dr Timothy Ball (a nephew of Philip Ball of the failed Mevagissey Bank), had been pressing for better sewage disposal and water supplies since the minor cholera outbreak in the village in 1832. However, he had met with little success because of the resistance of the principal landlords, one of whom was the Duke of Buckingham. It was later found that the Mevagissey epidemic was triggered by sewage leaking from a cracked pipe into the main village water supply.[3]

The role of church and chapel was of great importance during the cholera outbreaks. People invariably turned to religion in times of trouble and some clergymen played a valuable, even heroic, part in helping with the epidemic. In July 1849 services were held daily and sometimes twice daily at the Mevagissey Wesleyan chapel and many, it has been reported, 'found the Lord'.[4] Mrs Stephen Dunn of Mevagissey, who was ten in 1849, recalling the outbreak in old age, remembered going into the Wesleyan schoolroom when the plague was at its height and seeing people crying for mercy.[5] Depressing tracts relating to the outbreak were circulated advising people to 'Prepare to meet your death'. One warned, 'Fearful indeed are its attacks, sudden its striking. Life and health in the morning; death before night. Its special prey is the drunk and the fornicator, the filthy in body and the filthy in soul.'

The idea that the epidemics were a revenging plague sent by God to punish 'the filthy in body and filthy in soul' was widely accepted. In a sermon on cholera the Reverend Charles Kingsley put forward his theory that cholera was preventable. He went on:

But that does not prevent its being a visitation of God; yea, in most awful and literal earnest, a house-to-house visitation. God uses the powers of nature to do His work: Of Him it is written, 'He maketh the winds His angels, flames of fire His ministers. And so this minute and invisible cholera-seed is the minister of God, by which He is visiting house to house, searching out and punishing certain persons who have been guilty, knowingly or not, of the offence of dirt; of filthy and careless habits of living ...[6]

It would have been little comfort to the people of Mevagissey to know that the terrible disaster that had hit their town was their fault; many of them would have feared that anyway. Some church leaders hoped that the coming of cholera would lead to a wave of repentance and reform amongst the poor and a spiritual revival in the country. To a certain extent this did happen as people, especially in the affected areas, crowded into church and chapel. At one of the special services at the Mevagissey Wesleyan chapel during the outbreak, William Drew Lelean, a grandson of the Nicholas Lelean who had been imprisoned in France, was converted and subsequently spent his life converting the people of Van Diemen's Land, now Tasmania.[7]

The encampment of the inhabitants of Mevagissey at Portmellon, August 1849

This was not the first cholera epidemic in the British Isles. The first case had appeared in Sunderland in 1831, apparently brought there on a ship from Russia. By June 1832 the infection had spread over most of the country and 22,000 people had died.[8] In the 1848–9 epidemic, the one that affected Mevagissey, at least 50,000 people died in England and Wales. There were further outbreaks in 1854 particularly in London and in the Crimea, where 16,000 British soldiers died of cholera and other diseases. A London doctor, John Snow, famously removed the pump handle in Soho to prevent the local residents drinking contaminated water but a government inquiry concluded that his theory that cholera is waterborne was completely without foundation. It was not until 1883 that the virus was isolated from a sample taken from a water tank in Calcutta by Robert Koch. Following his findings vaccinations were introduced in the 1890s but not perfected until the 1920s. Mevagissey escaped further outbreaks even though the town was found to be as filthy as ever in 1853 and in 1866 there was an outbreak at the nearby china clay port of Charlestown.[9]

The government and local authorities had been endeavouring to discover ways to control the spread of cholera ever since the first outbreak in 1831. In mid-August 1849, the local doctors combating the disease in Mevagissey decided that something more had to be done and applied for help to the Board of Health, who obtained tents from the Ordnance, and these were erected at Portmellon on the side of a hill. On Wednesday 15 August about 200 people from Mevagissey took up residence in the tents. I have inherited the copy of a drawing of Portmellon which appeared in the *Illustrated London News* on 25 August under the headline 'Cholera at Mevagissey in Cornwall: Encampment of the inhabitants at Port Mellon'. The drawing looks across at the tents in the field and the various buildings from the south. A key indicates that the Inn was turned into a hospital and that the nearby cottages, Rock cottage, the block of fishermen's cottages and the house now known as the Anchorage housed the refugees and doctors. The Anchorage may well have belonged to Walter Williams by this time although the family were not yet living there.

Walter Williams, like many of the mariners, was at sea for most of this terrible period oblivious to the worry and stress that his wife and family were experiencing. The Williams were probably still living in Cliff Street, where many of the fishing community lived, and where more people died in the outbreak than in any other area. Thankfully the family survived but one of Walter Williams' very close friends, Walter Dunn, who had built the *Brilliant* for him, was one of the early victims. He was buried on 21 July, aged 60 years. In 1936 a slate headstone was found in the old Daubuz fish cellars recording the deaths of members of the Dunn family including three who had died within three days of each other from cholera. Matthias, a fisherman of 48, died on 10 August and his parents, Stephen and Mary, who were in their early seventies, died on 12 and 13 August. The Hunkin family, also fishermen and related to the Dunns, lost five people including three children, a grandmother of 82 and a young woman of 35.

On 17 July 1849 the fisherman Peter Furse, who had died from cholera at the age of 66, was buried and a stone erected in his memory in the churchyard. Others who died from cholera were buried in a huge communal grave on the edge of the churchyard. The stone for Peter Furse stands alone in the open grassy area of the otherwise

The area where the cholera victims were buried in 1849 with Peter Furse's headstone in the foreground

crowded graveyard. The poor, made poorer still by the epidemic, could not afford gravestones. 'I heard a voice from Heaven say come to me', the verse on Peter Furse's stone reads, 'for blessed are the dead which die in the Lord from hence forth, yea, saith the spirit that they may rest from their labours and their works do flow.'

Mevagissey was changed by the cholera outbreak. The town may have been used to sudden death from disease and accidents at sea but to lose six per cent of the population in two months was traumatic. People mourned the loss of their children, their mothers and fathers, their husbands and wives, their brothers and sisters, their friends and neighbours, and tried to adapt and rearrange their lives without them. By 1851 Elizabeth, the widow of Peter Furse, had moved to River Street to share a house with her son Peter, who was also a fisherman, and his family. There were ten people in the little house. She and her unmarried daughter, Mary, worked as fish curers, packing up the casks of fish for export. Her three oldest grandsons, Peter, John and Josiah, who were aged between 15 and 19, were already working as fishermen, probably in the same seine as their father. Three other grandsons, William, Israel and Samuel, were still at school. The emotional scars gradually healed as people came to terms with their loss and struggled to earn enough for their families to live on through the good years and the bad.

# A MERCHANT AND A
# GENTLEMAN OF MEVAGISSEY

*Trade is so far here from being inconsistent with a gentleman, that, in
short, trade in England makes a gentleman, and has peopled this nation
with gentlemen.*

DANIEL DEFOE, *The Complete English Tradesman*, 1725

O N THE 10TH January 1840 the local newspaper, the *West
Briton*, recorded that 'A fine vessel of 200 tons burthen, was
launched from the building yard of Messrs. Lelean and Co, at
Mevagissey, amid the hearty cheers of a great number of spectators.
The vessel is the *Elizabeth Mary Ann*, named after the lady of the
principal owner, and she reflects great credit on the builders.' The
principal owner was John Pearce the younger, a merchant of Mevagissey. He had married Elizabeth Mary Ann Morrice of Ryde on the Isle
of Wight in May 1836, when he was 44 and she was 35. He and his
father, John Pearce senior, were powerful men in the little community.
They were shareholders in many merchant vessels and seines, and
were closely involved with the buying and selling of fish and other
goods. They also owned a substantial amount of land and property
around the town, including fields, cellars and houses.

John Pearce senior had started out in business as a cooper. Much of
the economy of the area depended on the coopers who made casks
(hogsheads, puncheons, pipes) for wet and dry commodities, which
included beer, salt meat, pilchards, herrings and china clay. In
Mevagissey the demand was mainly for hogsheads (which had a
capacity of 52 gallons) for transporting pilchards. Stave-wood for the
casks was imported from the Baltic and cherry wood for the hoops
from France. John Pearce senior had married Elizabeth Jago, whose
father was Thomas Dalby Jago of St Mawes, the Agent and Trustee for

the Duke of Buckingham who owned most of the land to the west of the river in Mevagissey and even more in St Mawes. Houses and cottages at this time were usually held on lease from landlords like the Duke, the leases being for two or three 'lives'. On 24 April 1810 the Marquis of Buckingham, as he then was, gave John Pearce, merchant, a 99-year lease on a dwelling with garden and orchard in Mevagissey, which was determinable upon the deaths of his three children, John, who was then 19, Ann, 16, and Thomas, 8. The Marquis, as was customary, retained all timber and mineral rights and was paid a rent of ten shillings per year. Thus, early in the nineteenth century John Pearce had moved on from cooperage to become a merchant and gentlemen; his elevation helped by his propitious marriage and the profits of his involvement in smuggling and privateering. He had been the main shareholder of the disaster-prone *Seven Brothers* and when her captain, Nicholas Lelean, was in prison in France, he wrote regularly and sent money to him. Both men were stalwarts of the local Methodist church and when Nicholas Lelean wrote back to John Pearce he treated him with some deference, addressing him as 'My dear Sir' before subjecting him to long passages on his unswerving faith that the good Lord would look after himself and his family. John Pearce senior died in 1844. At 86 he had lived an unusually long life by nineteenth-century standards. His son, John, was the sole executor to his will, in which his father referred to himself as a 'gentleman of Mevagissey', and a major beneficiary with his sister, Ann, and the children of his brother Thomas.[1]

The merchants of Mevagissey bought and sold and their skill in these negotiations was crucial to success in business. Barclay Fox, of Falmouth, came frequently to supervise the landing of fish in Mevagissey for his family's company and to negotiate with the other people involved in the business. He wrote in his diary that on a lovely morning on 21 September 1839 he left Falmouth soon after eight o'clock and had a beautiful ride to Mevagissey, arriving there at half past eleven. He met his uncle at one of the curers and they prepared a 'whole lot of letters for our London friends [buyers], leaving a space for the price'. After dinner the curers and merchants congregated in separate rooms at an inn. There was a little haggling about conditions before the curers sent in their price, which was 70 shillings per hogshead. The merchants then sent in their offer which was 40 shillings. After some further

*Opposite*: Three ladies on Polkirt Hill overlooking Mevagissey harbour

107

Polperro fish market, *c.*1860 (Lewis Harding)

discussion the curers lowered their price to 60 shillings but this was not low enough for Barclay Fox and, as there was no prospect of a better price being negotiated, he took his horse and set out for home.[2] John Pearce was probably present at these negotiations either as a representative of the curers or as a buyer.

It was highly advantageous for a merchant to have his own ships to carry his merchandise, whether it was fish or clay or coal or any other product. Between 1834 and 1841 John Pearce the younger held shares in 10 vessels, two of them built by James or Walter Dunn and four by Nicholas Lelean and partners. In 1840 he had asked Nicholas Lelean to build him the schooner which he named *Elizabeth Mary Ann*, after his wife, and the next year he commissioned a brigantine which he called the *John Pearce*. He had life-like figureheads of his wife and himself made for these ships. In both ships he was the major shareholder, holding 16 or one quarter part of the shares. This was a new departure in his business and would have enabled him to ensure very favourable terms for the transit of his goods.

The major shareholder often acted as the manager for the ship. John Pearce the younger took on this role with several ships, including the *Elizabeth Mary Ann* and *John Pearce*, just as Samuel Allen had done for the *Brilliant*. In consultation with the master the manager would arrange the loading and discharging, the supplies, the repairs and the insurance of the ship. He would collect the freight charges and assist with customs, harbour masters and crews. He acted for the owners in finding cargoes and for charterers in finding suitable ships. He would buy and sell vessels, or shares in them, and act on behalf of others who wished to buy and sell shares and ships. He kept the accounts and reported at the regular shareholders' meetings. In return for his services the manager received such commission, brokerage or other returns as he could arrange. The business demanded an ever-changing knowledge of ships, their owners, masters and movements and of the trades for which they were suitable. But shipping was just one aspect of John Pearce's multifarious business activities in pilchards, seines, property and other miscellaneous goods.

In June 1850 John and Elizabeth Mary Ann Pearce left Mevagissey for a trip north. First of all, they travelled to Liverpool where they met their friend Thomas Jago, the Mevagissey-born merchant who had previously worked in Naples but was now based in Liverpool. The three of them were booked to travel to Glasgow, probably combining

The brigantine the *John Pearce* with luggers in Mevagissey harbour, 1875

### REDUCTION OF FREIGHTS AND FARES.

FREIGHTS TO AND FROM GLASGOW—Bale and Case Goods 3d. per foot; Cotton (American), 12s. 6d. per ton ; Ditto (Surat), 10s. per ditto ; Grey Calicoes for Printing, 2d. per foot.

The Glasgow and Liverpool Steam Shipping Company's new Steam-ship ORION......Captain HENDERSON ; The Glasgow and Liverpool Royal Steam-Packet Company's Steamer PRINCESS ROYAL...Captain CRAWFORD The City of Glasgow Steam-Packet Company's Steamer, ADMIRAL............................Captain HARDIE

are intended to sail (*with or without Pilots*) as under:—

### FROM (*Clarence Dock*) LIVERPOOL.

**JUNE.**

| | | | | |
|---|---|---|---|---|
| ADMIRAL | Saturday | 15, at | *4½ | Afternoon. |
| ORION | Monday | 17, at | 3 | Afternoon. |
| PRINCESS ROYAL | Tuesday | 18, at | 4 | Afternoon. |
| ADMIRAL | Thursday | 20, at | 7 | Evening. |
| ORION | Saturday | 22, at | 8 | Evening. |
| PRINCESS ROYAL | Monday | 24, at | *1½ | Afternoon. |
| ADMIRAL | Tuesday | 25, at | *1½ | Afternoon. |
| ORION | Thursday | 27, at | *2½ | Afternoon. |
| PRINCESS ROYAL | Saturday | 29, at | *4 | Afternoon. |

N.B.—Goods for Shipment on the days marked * must be alongside of the Ship Three Hours before appointed time of Sailing ; other days One Hour.

N.B.—The Steamers leaving Liverpool and Glasgow on Thursdays call at Ramsay Bay, Isle of Man, to land and receive Passengers, weather permitting.

FARES—CABIN, 10s.; Steward's Fee, 2s.; STEERAGE, 5s.

*Passengers are requested to take charge of their own Luggage, as the Ship is not responsible in any way for its safety.*

All Goods carried by these Vessels, and which are to or from the interior of England, &c., when consigned to the care of any of the Company's Agents in Liverpool, are forwarded, free of all charge for Forwarding, Cartage, and Dues at Liverpool.

AGENTS for the ORION,
T. MARTIN, and BURNS and Co.,
7, Water-street, Liverpool.

AGENTS for the ADMIRAL,
DAVID MACIVER and Co.,
12, Water-street, Liverpool.

AGENT for the PRINCESS ROYAL,
ROBERT LAMONT,
33, Water-street, Liverpool.

Advertisement for sailings of the *Orion* to Glasgow from the *West Briton*, June 1850

business with pleasure, in the Glasgow and Liverpool Steamship Company's fine new steamship the *Orion*. An iron vessel of 810 tons she had been built on the Clyde three years earlier and had a reputation for speed and comfort. She left Liverpool shortly after three o'clock in the afternoon of the 17th June with 160 passengers and a crew of 40.

The weather was calm and a smooth and rapid voyage was anticipated. After dinner the passengers went to their cabins to prepare themselves for bed. At a quarter to two in the morning everyone on board was suddenly woken by a violent judder. The ship had struck a sunken rock a short distance north of Portpatrick, on the Scottish coast immediately opposite Belfast Lough, and seconds later came to a complete standstill. As water began to seep into the cabins people ran out on to the deck in their night-clothes. The captain ordered the lifeboats to be lowered and as the passengers jostled and clambered to get into them the cry 'The ladies' went up. Those who could not get into the lifeboats clung to anything that floated. 'There was no undue clamour,' reported the *Liverpool Journal*, 'but a resolute effort for safety, or a religious resignation to their inevitable fate.' The ship sank a few minutes after she had struck. A survivor described how he held on to his wife as they were sucked down into the vortex of the sinking ship. He lost hold of his wife but within seconds she rose up and he managed to grab her and hold on to one of the ropes attached to the mizzenmast. After about half an hour a boat came from the shore to pick them up. On landing the passengers were taken to Portpatrick where the local people looked after them, finding them clothing and anything else they required.

This was a major disaster and the Liverpool, Scottish and national newspapers covered the story extensively. Amongst the list of survivors printed on 22 June in the *Liverpool Mail* was Mrs John Pearce; amongst the list of those who drowned were Mr John Pearce and Mr Thomas Jago. These two gentlemen had indeed allowed the ladies to go first. On the same day the *Liverpool Journal* had further news: 'The *Princess Royal* of Glasgow called at Portpatrick and arrived here yesterday bringing the following news, the people with diving apparatus had recovered luggage and other property, the number of bodies found to that time is 23, the entire loss will be under 40. She has brought the

bodies of Mr Jago, Mr Pearce and Mr Roby back to Liverpool.' When the newspapers had covered the human story they turned their attention to the ship and attempted to discover exactly what had happened and why. Why was the ship so close to the shore and why was the second mate on the bridge while the Captain and first mate slept?

The *Orion* steamship

The news took some time to reach Cornwall and it was not until 28 June that the *West Briton* reported the tragedy: 'Drowned by the wreck of the *Orion*, off Portpatrick, on the 18th instant, John Pearce, Esq., of Mevagissey. In his native town his loss will be sincerely deplored, as, on all occasions of difficulty he was at once appealed to by his suffering neighbours, anxious to be guided by his advice, and who promptly received from him in the hour of need that succour which the most unaffected benevolence could suggest.' There is no gravestone in his memory in Mevagissey churchyard; he was probably

The wreck of the *Orion*

buried in Liverpool. The body of Thomas Jago, however, was brought
back to Mevagissey and buried under a stone engraved with the
words, 'Sacred to the memory of Thomas Jago, merchant, who was
drowned the 18th June 1850 on his passage from L'pool to Glasgow
here interred on the 30th instant. Aged 58 years.'

In Mevagissey such a disaster would have been greeted with sadness but not surprise. As we have seen, shipwrecks and loss of life were
a part of people's lives and perhaps, as most of the local seamen still
relied on sail, there might have been a little satisfaction that those
'damned sea kettles', as they called the steam ships, were not infallible.

In other parts of the country stories of shipwrecks held a morbid fascination; the more dreadful and gory, the more popular they became.
Broadsides recounting the anguish of shipwrecked mariners as they
clung to rocks, unable to find food or water as the raging sea battered
the rocks below, were immensely popular. The story of the *Orion* was
written by one of the survivors, the Revd. J. Clarke, and published in
1851. It was illustrated by a dramatic lithograph showing the passengers
struggling on the upended ship and in the water. The scene as presented appeared both terrible and deeply romantic.

The Revd. J. Clarke described his book on the tragedy as 'a tribute
in gratitude', and his understandable gratitude for his survival, and
perhaps his calling, caused him to mask the drama of the disaster. Its

account is all too tame. More to the public's taste would have been the following story, told in laconic diarist's prose by Barclay Fox of Falmouth on 6 January 1836. 'A brig called the *Agenoria* arrived from St John's bringing 11 men, the crew of a timber vessel, who they had picked up in the most forlorn condition. They were capsized on the night of the 3rd December in a tremendous storm. Having cut the lanyards with much difficulty the vessel was righted & the crew, with the exception of 3 who were drowned, congregated on the quarter-deck. All their provisions were washed overboard and they continued till the 18th enduring the extremity of starvation and misery. On that day they came to the decision of drawing lots for who should die for his comrades & a young man of 19 was the victim. After prayers he took the knife and cut his arm across & across, but no blood appearing they cut his throat and drank the blood and devoured a considerable part of the body before it was cold. On the 20th another man being at the point of death, they cut his throat to save the blood & on the 24th another for the same reason. Having finished their horrible meal on that day a sail was discovered by the crew with tears of joy. This was the *Agenoria* which took them on board. They are now settled in two Poor-Houses where they are all likely to recover.'[3]

John Pearce's will, which he had made just nine months before he was drowned, was proved on 12 August 1850 in the presence of his wife Elizabeth Mary Ann, who was the sole executor.[4] It is a long document and immediately reveals that all was not well within his family. The very first words are: 'I am desirous to record in this first part my deep sorrow of heart that the disgraceful conduct of my nephew Wm. Britton Pearce has rendered it obligatory to me, as a matter of duty and as making my sense of his proving himself so devoid of all affection...to amend a will which I had made in his favour under the hope that he would have proved himself deserving of all that has been done for him and have done honour to the name of Pearce instead of disgracing it.' William Britton Pearce had been living with his uncle and aunt and grandfather in 1841 and, at the time of his uncle's death, was twenty-seven. He was the son of John Pearce's brother Thomas. And here another tragedy emerges for in 1836 Thomas had committed suicide, leaving his wife and three children to cope on their own. On 5 August 1836 the *West Briton* reported that an inquest had been held at Mevagissey on the previous evening on the body of Thomas Pearce, a merchant of that place. 'The deceased had been in a very despondent state for some months past, and about seven o'clock yesterday morning hung himself in a hay-loft adjoining his house.' The verdict, as was usual in cases of suicide, was 'insanity'. It seems likely that his older brother John, newly married, offered to look after Thomas's son. Later in his will John Pearce talks of the hundreds and thousands of pounds that have been spent on the young man. Perhaps John Pearce had sent him away to boarding school; perhaps he had bought him a commission in the army or navy; perhaps the boy had reacted against the strict routine of a devoutly Methodist family with no other children in the house. Either way he rebelled against his uncle and probably diverted himself with drinking and gambling and other pleasures.

There was another reason for John Pearce to rewrite his will. The late 1840s were a time of Railway mania with everyone being encouraged to invest in a venture that, it was believed, would bring great prosperity. John Pearce had been persuaded to invest in the Devonshire Railway but the shares had fallen so much that, he alleged, the value of his estate was halved. The will reveals a good deal about John Pearce's wide business interests, which included property in Plymouth and the Isle of Wight, and his status as a wealthy merchant in Mevagissey. He remembered his servants, laying aside the sum of £16 to be spent on suitable clothing (not black) for his oldest servants and those employed by him. To his wife he left the house they lived in with all the gardens and plantations and the Old Custom House and Quay in Plymouth. When she died this property was to go to his sister, Ann Slade, of 11, The Grove, Clapham Road, London. He left his cellars and premises with lofts and storehouse together with all the cellar materials and all the stock of fishery salt to his brother-in-law, John Slade. He also left him all the shares in his pilchard seines. To his sister-in-law Sarah Hopwood, who was living with him, he donated all the land known as the New Parks, Slade's Meadows and Bloody Field which comprised about five and a quarter acres. To his wife he gave all his shares in his ships, to hold or to sell as she saw fit, and he desired that John Slade take on the management of these vessels if it was agreeable to the majority of the owners. As he lived in Clapham that might have presented difficulties, but perhaps he returned to live in Mevagissey. To his wife John Pearce left all the objects that he had acquired as his wealth grew: household furniture, plate, books, wine, paintings and prints, linen and chaise and horses. He asked her to 'make such remembrances after my death to such friends as she will know it would be my wish' and to give his dear friend Mr Mills his silver watch and appendages, value £15, and to continue 'our little charities in my native place as far as her circumstances will allow.'

The story of the tragic death and will of John Pearce have been described in some detail because they reveal so much about business and family life in Mevagissey at the time. The merchants were the men with the money and therefore the power. The fisherman and the mariners danced to their tune. John Pearce was one of those who had not suffered from the fall of the Mevagissey Bank in 1824, although his subsequent investment in railways had proved disastrous. He was a Cornish version of Jolyon Forsyte in Galsworthy's *Forsyte Saga*, probably often to be seen strutting around the quays of Mevagissey wearing his top hat and, of course, his silver watch and chain.

# A DAM BAD OLD MAN

*'Sailor men 'ave their faults,' said the night-watchman, frankly, 'I'm not denying it. I used to 'ave them myself when I was at sea.'*

W.W. JACOBS, *The Lady of the Barge,* 'Bill's Paper Chase'

IN SPITE OF the problems Walter Williams had been experiencing with the *Brilliant* and the *Zuleika*, his reputation was apparently still high when he became the master of the *Elizabeth Mary Ann* on 21 May 1852. As we have seen, the *Elizabeth Mary Ann* had been commissioned from the Lelean yard in 1840 by John Pearce the younger, and named after his wife. James Ball was the first master, followed by Henry Lowry of St Mawes (1846 to 1849) and William James Olver (1849 to 1852).

*Opposite*: Walter Langford Williams, *c.*1870. (G. Ridsdale Cleare)

When Walter took over the *Elizabeth Mary Ann*, 120 tons, registered ship number 32991, he was 47 and had been the master of his own ship for twenty years. It is difficult to assess what kind of captain he was. The master was usually the only man on board with any knowledge of navigation and on an ocean voyage the ship and her crew were entirely dependent on him. However, the master could not manage the ship on his own and he was therefore, in turn, dependent on his crew. A good master would encourage his sailors and get them to work willingly. A bad master, and there were only too many of them, would resort to cruelty and violence in order to keep the sailors in order and force them to carry out their work.

There is no avoiding the fact that sailors had a terrible reputation on land. A shipping master of the period described merchant seamen as 'designing and ungovernable beasts' who, when ashore, spent their time with the lowest people that could be found, more or less in a permanent state of intoxication.[1] Months of living in confined quarters, with periods of frantic activity interspersed with longer ones of great boredom, invariably led to days of drinking and whoring the minute

they received their money. The streets of sailor towns around the world were filled with sailors in various stages of drunkenness. There were an irresistible number of convivial taverns, gin palaces, low class drinking houses and dance halls in which to pass their time on shore and spend their money. In Liverpool in 1841 there were 11,000 sailors belonging to the port and 2,272 drinking places. As soon as a sailor left his ship in port the notorious crimps were ready to pounce and lead him, who was only too willing, to the places where he could most easily be fleeced. When he had lost all his money, the obliging crimps were waiting to dump him aboard any ship requiring seamen.

Early in the nineteenth century clergymen and others charitably inclined began to take an interest in the seedy world of the sailor. Missionaries distributed tracts, prayer books and bibles amongst the sailors and turned some old ships into floating churches. Seamen's institutes, where sailors could read and talk and study, and improved sailors' homes were founded to provide accommodation in ports. The reformers fought the crimping system and preached the benefits of temperance. Walter Williams was, of course, a Methodist and it was likely that most of his Cornish crew members were as well. They would have observed the Sabbath and not worked on Sunday, except when at sea where it was vital to keep sailing. On the *Elizabeth Mary Ann*'s Agreement for 1858 the words 'No grog allowed' seem more proscriptive than the usual 'No spirits except at the Master's option'.

The government was concerned at the bad name British ships, masters and seamen were getting in foreign ports. On 1 July 1843 James Murray, of the Foreign Office, sent out a letter to the British Consuls in foreign ports requesting information on the British sailors in their ports. He asked them to report 'any incompetency of British ship masters to manage their vessels and their crews, whether arising from deficiency of practical knowledge and seamanship, or of moral character, particularly want of sobriety; also, to the different conduct of the crews.' His object in gathering this information was to demonstrate to the government the need for action in a situation that he felt was having a detrimental effect on the reputation of the British Merchant Navy. He was concerned that the poor seamanship and behaviour of British crews was giving advantage to foreign rivals whose merchant vessels were said to be well manned and navigated. The information sent to him from the Consuls must have shocked even James Murray. The

*Opposite*: Inside the Sailors' Home and Red Ensign Club. © NMM

Consul at Danzig regretted having to report that there was not a more troublesome and thoughtless set of men than the British seamen. He quoted a case where a valuable cargo had been loaded but the ship was unable to sail because of the absence of the master who was found, after seven days, in a brothel. The Consul at Pernambuco in Brazil reported that hardly a ship arrived from Britain without the seamen complaining to him of brutality, starvation and insulting language.[2]

The Act of 1844 attempted to remedy the situation and to improve life on board for both masters and sailors. No man would, in future, be allowed to serve on board a ship without a ticket bearing his name and description. This ticket had to be deposited with the master of the ship when the articles were signed and returned at the end of the voyage. The Act also introduced proper payment of wages, a compulsory supply of medicines and lime juice (to prevent scurvy) and regulated punishments for deserters and assaults committed on board ship. Discipline was further tightened up by an Act of 1850. Certain offences were to be punished by imprisonment for one to three months. They included wilfully damaging the ship's stores or cargo, assaulting a master or mate, disobeying lawful commands and neglect of duty. The master now had to keep an Official Log in which he entered any incidents on board relating to the behaviour of the crew, illness, injuries and deaths. Local Marine Boards were established at the principal ports. They were to oversee the examinations of sailors and establish Shipping Offices in their districts where seamen could be engaged to serve on ships and where advance notes of their wages could be issued to them. The Shipping Masters appointed to take charge of the offices had to see that the Articles of Agreement for the voyages between masters and their crews were in proper form, and that the crews joined at the agreed time. They were also responsible for the settlement and payment of seamen's wages at the end of the voyage, and for ensuring that they received a proper discharge.

It appears as if it was increasingly difficult for Walter to find a Mevagissey crew and he was forced to take on whoever was available. Inevitably, some of the men proved less than satisfactory. In September 1853 when he sailed the *Elizabeth Mary Ann* to Leghorn the only crew member from Mevagissey was his nephew, Philip, who had only recently finished his apprenticeship but was now promoted to boatswain and thus became responsible for the sails and rigging and

The brigantine
*Thomas Hughes* in a
storm, 1858, by
Nicolas Cammillieri

for summoning the men to duty. It seems that Thomas Young, a 40-year-old Durham man, deserted in London before they sailed and, in his place, Walter took on a nineteen-year-old Swede called John Maisner. He also had on board a seaman from Havana called Antonio Reas. Seamen's wages were scaled according to age and experience as well as the position they held on the ship. On this voyage the seamen were paid £2 15s. a month, Philip Williams, the very young boatswain, was paid £2 10s., John Maisner £1 15s. and the sixteen-year-old apprentice and cook, William Essery, just £1.[3] As wages were a major expense owners endeavoured to keep them as low as possible. However, if wages were too low the crew was less likely to be cooperative and well disposed towards orders from the master, mate and boatswain.

The *Elizabeth Mary Ann* left London on 19 September for Leghorn but, in very strong winds in the Channel, she collided with the *Mary Ann* of Lyme Regis and had to put into Portsmouth harbour having lost her port quarter bulwarks [ship's side above deck] and mainsail.[4] When the damage had been repaired the *Elizabeth Mary Ann* set out for Leghorn again and arrived there on 10 December. The ship and crew remained there, whether looking for return cargoes or waiting for better weather, until 8 February. A long period in harbour with nothing for the crew to do but tedious routine tasks such as painting, tarring and picking oakum was a recipe for unrest. A note from the Consul at Leghorn on the back of the Articles states that the two foreign crew members, John Maisner and Antonio Reas, had taken their clothes and disappeared without trace. Such behaviour was no longer an option for British seamen as they were unable to sail without their tickets which were held by the master. Walter managed to find two Glasgow seamen to take their place: John Gray and William Moher. These men also proved unsatisfactory and when the ship arrived at Hamburg on 12 April 1854 they were discharged by mutual agreement.[5]

The aim of my research so far had been to find out as much as I could about my great-great-grandfather, Walter Langford Williams, and his ship, the *Brilliant*. I had discovered a great deal about the many voyages he undertook to the Mediterranean, to America, the West Indies and Newfoundland, but almost nothing about the man himself. Tantalisingly, I had found a physical description of his brother and nephew but not of him. I had discovered fascinating information about Mevagissey, and some of the characters who lived there, but comparatively little about the Williams family. I had found accounts of life at sea in the late eighteenth and nineteenth centuries by other mariners but could only guess what life aboard Walter Williams' ships, the *Susanna*, the *Brilliant*, the *Zuleika* and the *Elizabeth Mary Ann*, was really like. One day, sifting through the Crew Agreements for Fowey ships at the National Archives, all that changed. As before, when I had first found the name Walter Langford Williams on a ship's document, I felt like standing up in the almost church-like silence of the National Archive Reading Room and shouting 'Eureka!'

Amongst the records for the year 1858 I came across an Agreement for a voyage of the *Elizabeth Mary Ann*, Master Walter Langford Williams, from Newport to Venice between 26 April and 27 September. Inside the single folded sheet of the Agreement was a book of the same size, titled OFFICIAL LOG BOOK FOR EITHER FOREIGN GOING OR HOME TRADE SHIP.[6] I thought at first that it was a traditional ship's daily log. I expected notes on the weather, the ship's position in the ocean and, when in port, details of the unloading and loading of cargo. I was disappointed, at first, to find no such details. It turned out that this 'Official Log' was the one introduced by the Act of

1850, in which the master had to list any problems he had with the crew including bad behaviour, illness or death. My disappointment turned to elation when I realised that the log was in Walter Williams' own hand-writing. Surely now I would get a feeling of what kind of ship's master he was and therefore be able to assess what kind of man he was.

Subsequently, I found other log books for the *Elizabeth Mary Ann* and although Walter Williams had his fair share of stubborn and recalcitrant sailors, some voyages were completed without incident and he was able to record 'Very Good' alongside the names of all his crew in the log book for both 'General Conduct' and 'Ability in Seamanship'. On other voyages some sailors were marked 'Good' and some 'Middling' – none received the very worst assessment, 'Indifferent'. Because the Official Log reveals so much about life aboard the *Elizabeth Mary Ann* I am reproducing the entries for the 1858 voyage in full, with a few spelling and punctuation changes for clarity.[6]

MONDAY MAY 24, 1.30 P.M. LAT. 41-40, LONG 17-30
Thomas Lowe was ordered by the Mate Mr John Ley to turn to, he replied 'what the hell must I turn to'. The Mate then told him to tar down the main topmast stay, which he refused to do and said 'you cannot make me do it'. A quarrel commenced. I went forward to stop it and ordered the said Thomas Lowe to tar down the said stay. He also refused to me to do it and went to get down on the windlass and soon afterwards went below for which he forfeit out of his wages 2 days pay and is also subject to imprisonment for one month.
Fine 3s. 4d.

MONDAY 7 JUNE AT 4 A.M. AT VENICE
Henry Pengott through carelessness in not making the end of the bucket rope fast properly let it go overboard and it was lost.
Value 10s. 6d.

SUNDAY JUNE 13 AT VENICE
Henry Pengott had liberty to go on shore until evening but did not return on board until Monday evening 24 hours after his liberty for which he forfeited out of his pay 6 days pay.
Fine 6s.

Thomas Lowe neglected to do what he was told and because he was told to do it again made use of very foul language and called me a dam bad old man for which he forfeit 2 days pay.
Fine 3s. 4d.

TUESDAY JULY 6 AT 3.30 P.M. VENICE
Thomas Lowe refused to do any work and said he should knock off altogether for which he forfeit two days pay.
Fine 3s. 4d.

TUESDAY JULY 6 AT 6.00 P.M. VENICE
Thomas Lowe went on shore without liberty. Returned again at about 6.30. I asked of him where he had been he replied that he had been on shore for his pleasure.

WEDNESDAY JULY 7 AT 7.00 A.M. VENICE
Thomas Lowe refused to go to work and went on shore without liberty at about 7.00 a.m. and did not return until about 7.00 p.m. for which he will forfeit 6 days pay and subject himself to 3 months imprisonment.
10s.

THURSDAY JULY 8, AT ABOUT 7 A.M. VENICE
Thomas Lowe refused to go to work and went on shore without liberty. Returned again about noon and said he would go to work for which he forfeit 3 days pay.
Fine 5s.

It is difficult to assess from this whether Walter Williams was harsh or Thomas Lowe stubborn and foolish but the evidence seems to show the master dealing with a recalcitrant man quite fairly. However, Thomas Lowe's anger and resentment must have nearly boiled over when he realised that his total fine amounted to £12. 15s. As he was earning only £2 a month he had lost more than 6 months pay. For the return voyage he would be working for almost nothing as the whole voyage took just 7 months.

What does all this tell us about Walter Williams? Unsurprisingly

Walter Williams' own version of these events gives a favourable picture of his role as a fair disciplinarian. There was no reason that these illiterate, rough seamen should feel the kind of loyalty towards him that his Mevagissey crews might have had. To them he was just another master working them too hard, paying them too little and giving them terrible food and too little free time in port. Some masters might have gained the crew's grudging respect but the system was against this. A ship would arrive at a port requiring two more seamen. The master would go down to the Shipping Office to see if there were any men available. He was in a hurry and had to take whoever was available and this was often the kind of disaffected, dissolute seaman portrayed in stories of the period. It would be interesting to know, though, just why Thomas Lowe called him a 'dam bad old man'. Probably it was just because he stood between Thomas Lowe's desires and the duties he had agreed in the Articles to carry out while he was on board the *Elizabeth Mary Ann*. My suspicion is that Walter Williams was fair and firm but that he drove himself, his men and his ship hard in order to achieve the aim of every master-owner of a vessel and make a profit.

Thomas Lowe is fined 3s. 4d. for calling Captain Williams 'a dam bad old man'. Log book of the *Elizabeth Mary Ann*, 6 July 1858

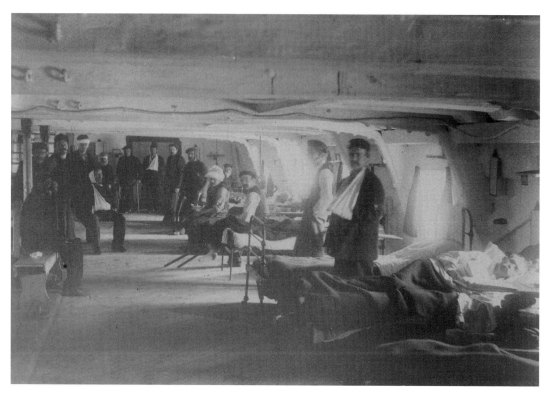

Patients on board the Hamadryad Hospital ship, Cardiff docks, nineteenth century

# ILLNESS AND DISEASE

*Smile glowing health!*
*For now no more the wasted seaman sinks,*
*With haggard eye and feeble frame diseased;*
*No more tortured longings for the sight*
*Of fields and hillocks green, madly he calls.*

W. BOWLES, *The Spirit of Discovery or*
*the Conquest of the Ocean*, 1804

ILLNESS AT SEA, or in foreign parts, in the eighteenth and nine-teenth centuries was a serious problem. In his book on seamen's missions Roald Kerndal described the plight of sailors who spent their days confined in their ship at sea: 'Cooped up in the dark, dank dungeon of a heaving forecastle, sailors succumbed all too easily to consumption, as well as other infections. His work place being his home – in fact, for weeks on end, his whole world – a seaman would be subject to the most severe stress and all too frequently, mental illness. Malaria, typhoid, yellow-fever, venereal disease, as well as miscellan-eous ailments relating to alcohol abuse, were rampant.'[1] Although a British naval doctor had discovered in 1753 that citrus fruit could both prevent and cure scurvy, the disease which had, in the past, taken the greatest toll of seafarers, there were no remedies for most diseases at this time. Seamen's missions were concerned about the number of men falling sick at sea and the number of ill and disabled seamen in ports and in 1821 the Seamen's Hospital Society was established to help the men of the Merchant Navy and fishing fleets and their depen-dants. However, most seamen continued to be treated in ordinary hospitals. The size of the problem can be gauged from the figures for 1865 for deaths at sea: 2,607 died from drowning or accidents and almost as many, 2,259, from disease.[2]

Philip Williams does not seem to have had the same drive as his

Havana harbour.
© NMM

youngest brother Walter. From 1836 to 1838 he was master of the *Churchill*, a 57 ton ship from Truro occupied mainly in conveying china clay from Charlestown to Liverpool and salt and general goods back to Southampton and Truro. Philip was qualified as a mate and master but did not sail regularly in any one ship. Like the casual crews that Walter picked up, he seems to have taken on whatever was on offer when he was free. In 1844, for example, he even acted as mate on the *Brilliant* under his younger brother, Walter. He does not appear to have ever owned shares in the ships he sailed in.

Philip had married Mary Over on 30 March 1830 and their first son, Philip, was baptised four months later on 1 August. Sadly, the baby boy died when he was only 10 months old. They had another baby boy on 1 July 1832 and he was also christened Philip and also died aged 10 months. The third baby Philip was baptised on 22 March 1835 and survived to become a mariner and boatswain on his Uncle Walter's ship, the *Elizabeth Mary Ann*. In 1837 Philip and Mary had another boy, John, who turned his back on the sea to become a shoemaker.

On 27 February 1854 Philip Williams took over from the regular master, Edward Hayes, aboard the *Kate*, a 66 ton Truro ship, when it sailed from Liverpool to Lisbon with a crew of six. Philip Williams was

128

now 54 and his mate, John Hancock of Mevagissey, was 52. On 1 May they were back in Bristol where the crew claimed their wages and were discharged.[3] Two weeks later Philip was already aboard another ship at Newport in Monmouthshire. He had taken on the position of mate of the large brig *D'Israeli* of Milford Haven, 225 tons. The master was Samuel James and there was a total crew of 9 men. The *D'Israeli*, named presumably after Benjamin Disraeli, the up and coming Member of Parliament who had become Chancellor of the Exchequer in 1852, had been registered at Milford in 1850. The ship left port on 18 May 1854 for Havana, Cuba. She arrived on 30 July and the crew unloaded the cargo. Twelve days later Philip Williams was dead.[4]

The British Consul General at Havana wrote on the back of the ship's Articles, 'I hereby certify that Philip Williams, late chief mate of the said Brig *D'Israeli* of Milford, died of Yellow Fever on 11 August in the Marine hospital of this harbour. I further hereby certify that the Master of the said Brig *D'Israeli* has in all things conformed to Act 7 & 8 Victoria Chapter CXII at this place.'[4] If the officials were matter-of-fact about death, seamen were more imaginative. In the yarns with which they whiled away time on board ship death featured as an event to be avoided with cunning and courage. Sailors with redeeming features ended up in a kind of fairyland under the sea called 'Fiddler's Green' while the rest were confined to 'Davy Jones's Locker', a euphemism for hell.

Philip Williams was one of thousands of sailors who died from the yellow fever in South America and Africa. It is said that in the nineteenth century one-third of the people of Havana died during the hot months each year from the disease. Like malaria, yellow fever is spread to humans by infected mosquitoes although this was not known in the nineteenth century. Another sailor, Frank Bullen, has written of his arrival at Havana at the time of an epidemic of yellow fever. The harbour was crowded with vessels that had lost members of their crew and flew the dreaded yellow flag denoting illness on board. He wrote that 'It was heartbreaking to see and hear the agony of sailors taken ashore to the hospital. They knew full well that there was hardly a glimmer of hope that they would return.'[5] Yellow fever victims began to feel ill a few days after being bitten by an infected mosquito and quickly developed a high fever, headache, muscle ache and vomiting. After a brief remission the infection led to shock, bleeding, liver and kidney failure and death. Liver failure caused jaundice and the yellowing of the skin and whites of the eye that gave the disease its name.

Philip's outstanding pay and effects were delivered to the local Shipping Master. The money, just £6 10s. 9d., was forwarded to the Board of Trade on 15 August. This was presumably then sent on to his widow, Mary, along with his effects which comprised a chest of sundries, a bag of sundries, a quadrant and a silver watch.[4] His clothes would have either been destroyed, if they were thought to be infected, or auctioned amongst the crew. His body would have been buried in Havana. Philip left no will but his son Philip would have inherited his quadrant and either he, or his brother, John, his silver watch.

A silver watch was a symbol of maturity and status and a valued possession in eighteenth- and nineteenth-century Mevagissey. There were no wristwatches of course; a watch was kept in a pocket or suspended across a waistcoat on a chain. Thomas Furse, after a successful season for pilchards in Mevagissey when 'The town was full of fish; money circulated in all directions', was able to purchase 1/16th part of a seine and a watch. These were, he wrote, 'the first two things that a careful young man in that place generally aspired to.'[6] When Thomas Ley, who had been the master of the *Brilliant* from 1849 to 1850, died in 1855 he left an unusually detailed will that revealed his close attachment to his calling. At his death he owned 28 shares in the *Freedom* and was able to leave four shares to his wife, Jane, and four to each of his six children. He left his charts and nautical books and instruments to his three sons to be divided equally. He gave a picture of the schooner *Freedom* to his son, James, and one of the *Grasshopper* to his daughter, Elizabeth. (A man who was a shareholder and a master of a ship and whose prosperity was intimately and entirely bound up in his vessel, felt close to his ship in a way that the poorly paid, hard pressed crew rarely did.) To his youngest son, Joseph, he left his watch and "appendage".[7]

George Boardley, who was Captain Williams' Bos'un aboard the *Elizabeth Mary Ann* in 1859, suffered from some kind of scurvy but also, it would seem from the Log record which records his erratic behaviour, from mental problems. On 16 September 1859 the crew of the *Elizabeth Mary Ann* met their captain at the Sailors' Home in Well Street in London in order to sign the Agreement for a voyage from London to Yarmouth and thence to Leghorn.[8] This appears to have

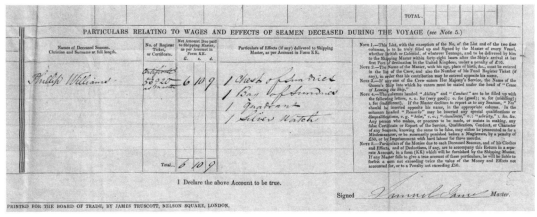

Philip Williams' pay and effects shown on the Agreement and Crew lists for the *D'Israeli* of Milford Haven, May–November 1854

been a difficult voyage from the start. For no obvious reason two members of the crew were discharged when the ship reached Yarmouth only a week after leaving London. Did the master or mate treat them too harshly or had they just cadged a lift to Yarmouth? Whatever the reason two more men joined at Great Yarmouth and the crew that sailed to Leghorn was as follows:

| Name | Age | Position | Birth place | Wage (monthly) |
|---|---|---|---|---|
| Walter Williams | 54 | Master | Mevagissey | |
| John Burnell | 39 | Mate | Devon | £4. 10s. |
| Thomas Nabrok | 24 | Seaman | Brazil | £1 5s. |
| Hendrik Stradman | 19 | Seaman | Hanover | £1 15s. |
| Thomas Lankman | 17 | Cook | Lowestoft | £1 |
| George Boardley | 31 | B'sun | Lowestoft | £3 |
| John Hollingsworth | 18 | Seaman | London | |

All went well for the first three weeks but on 18 October at 4.00 a.m. the Log records that George Boardley ' knocked off duty and went below being very unwell in a breaking out all over the body with a kind of scurvy. Took a dose of salts and rubbed his body with olive oil.' Walter Williams reported the course of George's illness in the Log Book;[8]

OCT 23 (AT SEA)
George still remains sick. Taking salts occasionally.

OCT 28 (AT SEA)
George still sick taking medicine occasionally.

NOV 1, 2 P.M. AT LEGHORN
Sent George to the Hospital.

SATURDAY NOV 12 AT LEGHORN
Discharged George Boardley at the consul's office not being in a fit state of health to remain in the ship.

DEC 27 ABOUT 11 A.M. AT LEGHORN
George Boardley came on board and borrowed some clothes from some of the other men saying that he had come out of the Hospital without Liberty, and that he had not sufficient clothes on to keep him warm.

At 3.00 p.m. the consul sent for me and told me he was very much surprised at the Man leaving the Hospital in such a way and said he must go back again and while we was talking a Man brought a note from the Hospital which the Vice Consul read some portions to me stating that he had taken advantage of some people coming in to see their friends and had deserted the Hospital. The Vice Consul stamped his foot and said he must go back again to the Hospital and that he would not get the Doctor's certificate unless he went back again or go to the doctors residence which would be very expensive. The man cried and said he would rather do anything than go back to the Hospital again. He would rather pay for lodgings himself. The consul said how could he pay for lodgings, he had no money. The man said he would be ill-used for running away. The Consul said if anyone ill-used him to tell him of it. I said I would give him half a dollar rather than he would be ill-used. The Consul said he must go back again and tomorrow at 12 o'clock he would meet me to go on board the *Terrible* and hear what the Doctor of the Frigate say, whether he is fit to go the voyage or not. Accordingly I was there at 12.00 p.m. but the Consul had not been there. I remained in the office until 1.30 p.m. When the Vice Consul came and said I must wait some 2 or 3 days while he would see some of the Doctors and ascertain if the man was fit to proceed as a seaman in the vessel or whether he must send him home passenger. I called several times but could not get any satisfactory answer until the 3 January when I said I was going to sea, he then said he was fit to go and sent him on board and charged me with all the expenses which I objected to.

132

At sea on 13th February Walter had more trouble with poor George Boardley. Food, as so often on board ship, was the catalyst for a near mutiny. At noon George called a meeting of all hands to talk about 'pease' [a pudding made from boiled peas]. Apparently, in very stormy weather, the cook had spilt all the pease into the fire. George shouted that the master should beat the cook for this mishap or let him do it. Walter Williams replied that he would not take the law into his own hands and that the crew must make the best of it. George then flew into a rage and threatened to come into the master's cabin and take his food. Walter told him to touch it if he dared whereupon George pulled off his things in a great hurry and put himself in a fighting position and said 'Now one dog one bone' and some more very 'mutinous language'. Walter told him that if he had come to him in a proper manner he could have had some of his food. George then sulked and said he would do no more work as he had sore feet. When his watch was called he came on deck and laid on a sail. Walter asked him how he was and he said that his feet were very bad and he knew what he wanted, he wanted rest and rest he would have. However, the next day he appeared to have miraculously recovered both his health and his temper. He took the wheel for an extra hour for the master and carried out his other regular work. Walter commented: 'So you see that a man who had his feet so sore that he could not turn out nor stand on his legs for about 22 hours is able and willing to stand an hour longer than his term, without making any complaint or saying that his feet is better or worse, and just after he called his meeting [about the pease] he put himself in a fighting attitude and almost challenged to fight one or more, and to take victuals by force and would not as much as ask whether he might have them or not.' It must have been a relief to Walter when, after six months with George Boardley, the ship docked at Gravesend on 1 March 1860.

The topsail schooner *Heligan* off Palermo

# THE ELIZABETH MARY ANN

*A merchant ship is built for one purpose only: to make money, to pro-*
*duce, like any other piece of machinery, a reasonable return on capital*
*invested.*

BASIL GREENHILL, Introduction in Gardiner, Robert (ed.)
*The Advent of Steam: The Merchant Steamship before 1900*

THE BUSINESS side of a merchant sailing ship could be just as risky as the navigational side. The ship was usually managed by a managing owner who was a major shareholder in the ship and chosen by the other shareholders. The *Brilliant* and *Zuleika* had been managed by Walter Williams' friend and fellow-Methodist, Sam Allen. The *Elizabeth Mary Ann* had been managed by John Pearce until his death and then by his brother-in-law, John Slade, as specified in his will. From March 1853, however, the *Elizabeth Mary Ann* was probably managed by Walter Williams himself. There were clearly great financial advantages for the master if he managed his own ship. The payments that would have gone to the owner-manager for looking after the business side of the ship would come to him and he would have greater freedom to choose his own routes and cargoes. On the other hand, he would have to take on the extra work of keeping full and accurate accounts and reporting to the shareholders.

Voyages rarely went smoothly. The weather was unpredictable and wayward and so, very often, were the crew. The precious cargo, the main source of income, frequently caused anxiety. The master had to ensure that the ship was loaded evenly and safely and that the cargo remained dry and in good condition. Oranges and other fruit, for example, would often rot, and coal occasionally caught fire. Once the ship reached a foreign port it was the master's responsibility to find either a return cargo or one for onward shipment as quickly as possible, for time spent in harbour was time spent without income.

When Hilary Marquand of Guernsey became a master in 1849, aged only 23, he quickly found that as well as looking after the ship for her owners he was also required to act as their agent. In his new role he had to arrange freights with merchants and brokers at home and abroad and was soon aware of the devious methods they used to get the best possible deal for themselves. He found that brokers were skilled at extracting handsome commissions for themselves whilst merchants were adept at adding misleading amounts to their accounts under such categories as 'Custom House Charges' or 'incidental and petty expenses'. The former were invariably bribes paid to the Customs officials to allow them to smuggle in their next importation from Europe, and the latter covered generous amounts of wine and cigars for themselves.[1]

As we have seen, business at this time was closely connected with a person's network of family links and friendships. Walter's fellow Methodists, who shared his religion and attitude to business, formed an invaluable and reliable group of close contacts. Sam Allen, Walter Dunn, James Dunn, John Pearce and the Lelean family were all Methodists and all worked closely with Walter Williams. He also had links with Thomas Jago when he was working in Naples and Liverpool, and with Thomas's brother, William, in Leghorn.

Walter's efforts to build up his shareholding in the *Elizabeth Mary Ann* illustrate the lively dealing in ship's shares that took place in a small sea port such as Mevagissey in the nineteenth century. Elizabeth Mary Ann Pearce, for whom the *Elizabeth Mary Ann* had been named, had inherited 15 shares from her husband, John, when he had drowned in Scotland in June 1850. Once more Walter was in the right place at the right time. On 17 March 1853, less than a year after taking over as master of the *Elizabeth Mary Ann*, Walter Williams was able to buy 7 shares from Elizabeth Pearce and thus become one of her major shareholders. He gradually built up his holding, buying more shares whenever someone was willing to sell and he had the funds available, until in 1866 he held 28 shares. After his retirement, Walter continued to manage the *Elizabeth Mary Ann* and on 17 April 1866 he mortgaged his 28 shares to John Eskett Lever, the new master of the *Elizabeth Mary Ann,* for £318 15s. plus interest. The shares in 1866 were therefore valued at about £11 3s. each. Walter continued to manage the ship until 6 July 1872 when he discharged the mortgage to John Eskett Lever.[2]

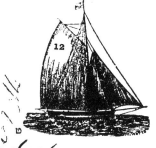

# INWARD CERTIFICATE.

No Pilot is allowed to receive any Perquisite, Fee, or
Gratuity whatsoever, either directly or indirectly, on
pain of Fine or Dismissal from the Service.

𝕿𝖍𝖎𝖘 𝖎𝖘 𝖙𝖔 𝖈𝖊𝖗𝖙𝖎𝖋𝖞 to the Owners or Agents of the *Snowdrop*
of *Fowey* from *Trieste*
drawing *10* Feet of Water, that *William Corbin*
a Licensed Pilot for the Port of Liverpool, belonging to the Pilot Boat **No. 12,** hath conducted
the said Vessel from *Bell Buoy* through the
*Victoria* Channel, into the Port of Liverpool, and brought her into a Dock or Place
of Discharge, and is entitled to Pilotage according to Act of Parliament.

      Witness my hand, the *11th* day of *March* 1843

Extra Days, *No the Maiden Bank*

*Queen Docks*

*John Lehan*

T. Kaye, Printer.

It is difficult to establish what kind of return the shareholders received on their initial investment. Surviving accounts indicate that the dividends paid to shareholders varied greatly. The master of the *Bess*, a schooner of 92 tons trading from 1840 to 1844 from Plymouth, owned 26 shares and earned just over £83 a year in dividends in addition to his wages.[3] The captain of the *Magic*, a schooner of 119 tons trading from Penzance between 1833 and 1839, owned 16 of the shares and earned an average of £31 a year over twelve voyages.[4] In other words, the interest earned on each share from the *Bess* was about £3 and from the *Magic* about £2 a year over those periods. These figures correspond with the rather later accounts for the schooner *Maggie C* which show that from 1877 to 1887 the shareholders of this ship received between 10s. and £4 each year, averaging at nearly £2 per annum.[5] These were not great profits but provided a welcome supplement to the wages of the ships' captains and at least some return for the other investors.

The main business activity of a ship was, of course, not in share dealing but in freight. As we have seen, Mevagissey ships had for centuries taken pilchards to the Mediterranean. In the nineteenth century

Pilot certificate for the *Snowdrop* at Liverpool, 11 March 1843

137

they also increasingly delivered manufactured goods from the rapidly expanding ports of London, Liverpool and Glasgow. Although steam ships were beginning to take over some freight routes, sailing ships still had a role as they were, at least to start with, more reliable and cheaper. Steam ships were three times more expensive to build than sailing ships and the coal required to create the steam was not only costly, it also took up cargo space.

The local product that the *Elizabeth Mary Ann* and the other Mevagissey ships most often transported from Cornwall at this time was china clay. This was quarried in the area around St Austell, taken to the local ports of Charlestown, Par, Pentewan and Fowey by cart or rail and then by ship to Gloucester, Liverpool, Runcorn and other ports at home and abroad. On 9 September 1841 the Customs Bill of Entry at Liverpool showed that the *Brilliant* had arrived at Liverpool with 75 tons of china clay, 40 tons of china stone and 10 tons of iron. In 1848, the *Brilliant* took 15 tons of scrap iron, 16 bales of bone and 10 tons of iron from Belfast to Liverpool and in 1861 the *Elizabeth Mary Ann* carried a load of chains, shackles and anchors, rod and bar iron from Glasgow to Liverpool.[6]

Political events and new government legislation, especially if they impinged on fishing or maritime endeavours, inevitably had some impact on the people of Mevagissey in spite of their isolation. In 1854 the only European war to be fought between the end of the Napoleonic Wars in 1815 and the Great War in 1914 broke out in the Crimea. During the war the government chartered many ships to transport the goods required by the army. The transport ships also took out soldiers and brought back the wounded.

On 1 December 1855 Walter Williams and the *Elizabeth Mary Ann* sailed from Naples to Gallipoli. On 28 January 1856 they arrived back in Mevagissey with sails split and other damage.[7] After emergency repairs the ship proceeded to Bristol. By the end of 1855 fighting had ended in the Crimea and this voyage may have had nothing to do with the war; Walter Williams may have been simply bringing home dried fruit from Gallipoli. However, it seems likely that on this and his next voyage, which was from Cardiff to Constantinople, the *Elizabeth Mary Ann* was chartered as a transport ship by the government. She arrived in Constantinople on 3 May with a number of other ships from Cardiff, which seems to indicate that they sailed in convoy.[8] On the return journey his final destination was an unusual one for him: Ipswich. Had he perhaps taken out equipment or food for the troops? Had he perhaps returned with some troops? The fact that this was his first visit to Constantinople seems too much of a coincidence for him and his ship not to have been involved in the war and its aftermath in some capacity or other.

It is rarely possible to discover what goods were exported by individual ships but lists of goods entered for exportation were regularly published by the Customs at Liverpool. These give some idea of the kind of goods exported to the places that Walter Williams travelled. For example, a list of goods bound for Naples on 16 August 1864 included 9 bales cottons, 1 bale worsted, 3 crates lathes, 11 cases hoop tyres and 8 crates hardware.[9] Liverpool was the main port for the industrial Midlands and Lancashire and the majority of the products exported were the manufactured goods of the English Industrial Revolution: woollen, linen, silk and cotton fabrics, glass, iron and tin goods, toys, cutlery, leather goods, agricultural implements and even straw hats.

The main imports that Walter Williams brought from Italy were the same romantic-sounding products that Britain imports from Italy today. In January 1855 the *Elizabeth Mary Ann* arrived in Liverpool from Leghorn with a large and varied cargo which included olives, alabaster, hemp, waste silk, blocks of marble, anchovies, olive oil, rags, linen, grass seed, boracic acid, argol and, rather surprisingly, a guitar.[10] Many of the imports were the raw materials required for manufacturing processes in the Midlands; from Palermo Walter Williams brought valonia, (oak acorn cups used in tanning, dyeing and making ink), brimstone (sulphur) and shumac (a shrub used in tanning, dyeing and medicine). Walter often brought back a cask of olive oil or other goods, such as figs or honey, for himself. The containers for the various goods included chests, bags, boxes, casks, pipes and pots. Marble and alabaster came as blocks or slabs. As well as listing the goods and their quantities, the Customs Bills of Entry also listed the merchants who had ordered the goods.

On Thursday, 5 February 1861 Walter Williams arrived in Bristol after one of his usual winter voyages. The *Elizabeth Mary Ann* had left London for Leghorn on 11 October and had therefore been away for nearly four months. The list of goods the *Elizabeth Mary Ann* landed at Penzance and Bristol is given in full below as well as the names of the merchants who were dealing with the goods.

## CUSTOMS LIVERPOOL
### CUSTOMS BILL OF ENTRY

*Ships reported inwards*
*Wednesday 5 February 1861*

ELIZABETH MARY ANN of Fowey, Williams
LEGHORN
120 tons J.Edwards & Co

| GOODS | MERCHANTS |
|---|---|
| 8 casks 20 boxes olive oil | T.A Warren |
| 100 hf chests      " | " |
| 100    "       " | E. Jones |
| 100    "       " | Manning, Hayman & Baker |
| 12 brls anchovies | Webb Brothers |
| 2 pipes, 55 hf chests olive oil | Longman & Co |
| 2 pipes, 5 qtr casks    " | S.G. Clements & Co |
| 45 hf chests      " | " |
| 2 pipes, 8 qr casks   " | Colthurst & Co |
| 50 hf chests      " | " |
| 44 slabs marble | J. Edwards & Co |
| 15 blocks of marble | Tyley & Son |
| 10 cases, 1 box alabaster | A.O. Jabi |
| 1 case olive oil | W. Williams |
| 1 box parmesan cheese | Order |
| 5 boxes macaroni | " |
| 24 boxes anchovies | " |
| 27 bales rags | " |
| 3 pipes, 17 hf pipes olive oil | Landed at Penzance |
| 9 qr casks       " | " |
| 760 hf chests 40 boxes " | " |
| 9 qr casks       " | " |
| 1 box essence | " |
| 8 cases macaroni | " |

Every item imported or exported had its own freight price, which varied according to supply and demand. It is difficult to draw any conclusions from the freight figures that have survived as they fluctuate so much. Some figures for a small home trader, the *Batten Castle*, operating between 1852 and 1866, show that cargoes of clay averaged 6 shillings and 9 pence per ton.[11] Walter Williams' cargoes of china clay (counting the same rate for the clay and clay stone) therefore brought in about £39 on each voyage. However, figures for the *Amelia* of Salcombe between 1824 and 1827 show clay freights averaging nearly double this rate at about 12 shillings a ton.[12] Ships from Salcombe, in Devon, specialised in the transport of oranges from Spain and the Azores. The captains of the fruit schooners brought the fruit back as quickly as possible because fresh and undamaged cargoes were rewarded by high freight rates and bonuses.[12]

In the mid-nineteenth century there were at least ten merchant ships owned and usually crewed by Mevagissey men. Nearly all of them followed similar routes to Walter Williams', sailing most frequently to

Horses loading slate from Delabole at Port Gaverne

the Mediterranean but also to the Baltic, Newfoundland, America and the West Indies. The *Snowdrop*, which has already been mentioned in Chapter 9, had been built by Nicholas Lelean in 1833 and at 116 tons she was larger than the *Brilliant* but a similar size to the *Elizabeth Mary Ann*. She sailed with a crew of six or seven. On 1 July 1842 Richard Nicholls of Mevagissey sold his ten shares in the *Snowdrop* to John Lelean, master mariner, for £250. The other main shareholders were the ubiquitous John Pearce the younger, merchant, and William Robins Trewavas, a mariner, both of Mevagissey. The account book for 1842 survives and provides some fascinating insights into the organisation and financing of a Mevagissey merchant ship of the time.[13] Freight provided the main income and from this the crew and master had to be paid (at rates of between £1 and £5 a month) and fed, the ship had to be kept in good order and repaired as necessary and payments made for loading and unloading and other charges in port covered.

In Naples on 6 October 1842 the master of the *Snowdrop*, John Lelean, paid Mr Antonio Deluces £34 18s. 5d. for sundries, probably food. He also paid one man six shillings for helping to discharge the cargo. On 10 October at Messina he paid the following charges:

| | | |
|---|---:|---:|
| Pilotage in | 17s. | 0d. |
| Discharging ballast | 14s. | 0d. |
| 25lb sugar at 6d pr lb | 12s. | 6d. |
| 26lb fish | 6s. | 0d. |
| Mr James Morrison for sundries | £35  12s. | 1d. |
| John Bonanna, waterman for bread, beef and Port charges | £20  13s. | 11d. |
| TOTAL | £58  15s. | 6d. |

Back in Liverpool on 5 March he had to pay three men 8s. for hobbling, that is for towing the ship along to her mooring, 8s. to the pilot and over £3 to the men who helped to unload the cargo. He also did a certain amount of ship maintenance, which may indicate that there had been some stormy weather on his return journey from Sicily. He paid £6 for caulking and mending the jiboom, 9s. for leather for the main sheet strap, £4 for rope and tar and £1 1s. for a compass and a lamp. Further accounts for 1848 indicate a turnover of £970 for the year, including a total of £678 received for freight. The crew was paid between 40s. and 50s. a month and was only paid for the time they had spent on the ship. The master, John Lelean, was paid £5 a month for the whole 12 months, a total of £60. His mate at this date was James Jolly, who was paid £35 for over eight months on board. The total bill for wages was £203 14s. 6d. Accounts for 1840–44 also survive for the schooner *Bess*, 92 tons, which traded from Plymouth, and these show that the percentage cost of the outgoings spent on victualling and wages was 29 per cent while the disbursements at port accounted for 55 per cent.[14]

I wanted to try and find out how much Walter Williams earned as a master/manager. I drew up tentative figures based on the fact that if he was paid £5 a month as a master then as a master manager, taking a proportion of the earnings on freight, he must have earned more, perhaps £6 or £7 a month, although of course this would fluctuate greatly depending on his cargoes. In addition to this he was receiving about £2 a year on each of his shares and as he ended up with 28 shares in the *Elizabeth Mary Ann* he would be earning £56. He might also have earned other money from commission, brokerage and the like.

| 1860 | Earnings per year at, say, £6 10s. a month | £78 |
|------|--------------------------------------------|-----|
|      | Share dividends (£2 each on 28 shares)     | £56 |
|      | TOTAL                                       | £134 |

I found a web site on which it is possible to compare earnings from any nineteenth-century date to 2006.[15] This revealed that the £134 Walter earned in 1860 was the equivalent of £81,463 in 2006, which means that he was earning a considerable amount. In contrast, his sailors might earn, if they were able to get continuous employment, about £24 a year, which is the equivalent of £12,903 a year in 2006.

Sam Allen and Walter Williams, in common with most shipping managers in the south-west, followed local tradition in their business dealings, preferring to deal with new situations and emergencies as they arose rather than laying down long-term plans. The ship-owners of Mevagissey were rarely entrepreneurs and only a few, such as John Pearce the younger, invested in more than one ship. They simply did not have the capital to build up fleets of ships like the Henleys and other large ship-owning firms in London and Liverpool. However, it may be that Sam Allen, the only man to describe himself as a 'ship-owner' in the 1851 Census for Mevagissey, aspired to own several ships when he purchased the *Zuleika*. John Pearce the younger, who held shares in many local ships and owned cellars in Mevagissey and a warehouse in Plymouth, was really first and foremost a merchant. He invested in ships in order to facilitate his fish-curing and other businesses and shrewdly spread his investments over a number of ships in order to reduce the risks. If a local man aspired to expand his business he usually left Mevagissey to work in one of the expanding ports of the north-east or abroad, as several of the Jago family had done. Hilary Marquand, the young master mariner from Guernsey mentioned above, moved from his home to Cardiff in 1870 and became a ship-broker and ten years later a ship-owner.[16] However, in common with other master/owners in the south-west Walter Williams probably never sought to do more than work hard to get the best return he could from the ship he captained. Although he must have been intelligent and well-organised in order to manage his ship, he lacked the time, as well as the capital, to expand further.

The risks associated with shipping meant that it always provided an uncertain living. A historian of the period has described it as a typical subsistence industry with little propensity for economic growth or development.[17] The aspiration of most ship's masters was to provide a good living for themselves and their families and to accumulate enough wealth to build themselves a house for their retirement. This Walter did achieve and with it a perceptible enhancement of his social standing in the local community. His achievement should not be underestimated.

# THE ANCHORAGE, PORTMELLON

*When men come to like a sea-life, they are not fit to live on land.*
SAMUEL JOHNSON

THERE IS A FEELING of light and space as one nears Portmellon after the dark, enclosed, winding streets of Mevagissey. Even now that retirement and holiday homes have filled the gaps at Portmellon between the old inn, the fish cellars, ship-yards, farms and mills, the little cove retains the atmosphere of the fishing and ship-building village that it was in the nineteenth century. Once part of the Bodrugan estate to the south of its stream and the Penwarne estate to the north, it is now split between Gorran parish and Mevagissey parish. Early in the twentieth century a road was built along the seafront and holiday homes and guest houses rapidly spread along it from Mevagissey, turning Portmellon into a virtual suburb of its larger

Oxen at Portmellon, 1893. The Anchorage is on the far right.

neighbour. But on the days that the sea lashes across the road the little hamlet is once again cut off from its more populous neighbour.

There is no doubt that the sea, potentially a cruel and deadly foe, had been good to Captain Williams and he had prospered. He had taken his family from a fisherman's cottage in Cliff Street to a house in Fore Street and finally to the Anchorage, an attractive villa on the cliffs at Portmellon. My mother's note had linked her great-grandfather with the site from 1820 when she wrote that its value was £50. I have not been able to discover when Walter Williams bought the site but, assuming that her note is true, it seems likely that he bought the land (perhaps with a small fisherman's or farmer's cottage already on it) in 1820. Over the years, when he had time between his long voyages, he transformed it, or employed others to transform it, into the stylish residence which in 1850, according to my mother's note, was valued at £500.

The house must have been finished by 1849 when it was shown in the *Illustrated London News* engraving of the cholera tents at Portmellon, looking much as it does today. The only other reliable information that I have been able to find to help determine when the Williams family moved to Portmellon is that provided by the ten-yearly censuses. In the 1851 Census Walter's wife, Ann, was living in Fore Street, Mevagissey, with her five children and a house servant. On 7 April 1861, the date of the next Census, the family were at Portmellon. Once again Ann, now 52 years old, was on her own with just two of her children, Jane, 23 and Sophia, 11. Walter was nearing Barcelona on a voyage from Bristol.

Walter had started his working life as a joiner but in 1828, aged 22, he had gone to sea and spent the rest of his life as a mariner. In retirement he and his wife kept a shop, just as his mother had done. They managed the shop from at least 1856, when Walter appears in Kelly's Directory as a Master Mariner/Shopkeeper. It was a business that the family ran for many years because Walter is recorded in the Post Office Directory of 1873 as a 'shopkeeper' and in Harrods Directory of 1878 as a 'general dealer'.

In his last few years at sea Walter made three long voyages to Newfoundland. These were part of one of the triangular routes regularly followed by merchant ships. They usually carried general goods out to Newfoundland, fish from Newfoundland to Lisbon and other parts of the Mediterranean, returning to England with oil, wine and fruit. On 10 July 1865 Walter set out from Liverpool for Newfoundland. His motley crew included a 17-year-old apprentice: his only son, Walter Williams Junior. This does not appear to have been a happy voyage. On arrival at St John's, four of the crew deserted and the replacements then recruited at St John's later also refused to sail with the *Elizabeth Mary Ann*. It appears that Walter Williams then took the decision to sail 80 miles north to Twillingate with only the mate and his son. Here he managed to find a crew and, loaded up with fish, sailed on to Lisbon where he arrived on 20 November. A month later, on 16 December 1865, Walter sailed the *Elizabeth Mary Ann* into Teignmouth harbour and, after unloading his cargo, proceeded to Mevagissey.[1] The voyage to Newfoundland had lasted 5 months and after 13 years with the *Elizabeth Mary Ann* and 33 years as a master, it was Walter Williams' last. He was nearly 60 and a year earlier, on 29 July 1864, he had been granted a pension for his years of service in the merchant navy.[2] There was no retirement for the *Elizabeth Mary Ann*; she sailed on under various masters until 11 January 1887 when she was stranded on the Chit Rocks off Sidmouth in a gale and wrecked. The *Elizabeth Mary Ann* must have been a strong, well-built ship; she had sailed the high seas for 48 years, since being built in 1839, an unusually long life for a deep sea vessel.

Ann Williams had adapted to spending most of the year without her husband whilst he was at sea. After his retirement they were spending all and every day together, although presumably one or other of them would be occupied in minding the shop. In 1866, in the year after Walter's retirement, their oldest daughter, Jane (my mother's 'Granny Pearce') married William Pearce. The young couple set up home in Mevagissey, where their first child, John Francis, or Frank as he was always known, was born in 1867. They had six more children who were all born at Tregerrick, the small farm they ran at Gorran. Ann was not able to enjoy either Walter's retirement or her first grandchild for long because on 26 March 1869 she died. She was only 61 years old.

There were great celebrations in Portmellon on 2 October 1869 and, for once, Walter Williams was at home and able to be involved in a major local event. A committee had been convened to organise the building of a lifeboat house at Portmellon and the arrival of the lifeboat. Walter was, jointly with William Roberts, the Secretary of this

The launch of first
Mevagissey lifeboat
at Portmellon, 1869

committee. John Tremayne, of Heligan, was the Chairman.[3] The fact
that a photograph of the launch survives within the family may indicate
that Walter is one of the men shown in it. Then, as now, the heroic feats
of men who risked their lives to save the lives of others inspired both
seafaring people and landlubbers to support them generously and the
first Mevagissey lifeboat was the gift of Sir Robert N.C. Hamilton,
Bart, K.C.B., and others from the Birmingham area. The lifeboat's
journey to St Austell station was paid for by the railway and from there
it was drawn on a carriage by 8 horses. Led by a band, it processed
through the streets of Mevagissey, which were decorated with banners
and bunting, to Portmellon.

A crowd of between three and four thousand people gathered to
watch the launch. After the Vicar had said a prayer and the local
schoolchildren sung a hymn for those at sea, the Honourable Mrs
Tremayne performed the launching ceremony and named the boat the
*South Warwickshire*. The lifeboat, which was powered only by oars
and sail, was then brought round to Mevagissey harbour where,
amidst much cheering and applause, the crew demonstrated the boat's
self-righting abilities.[4] The festivities concluded with tea in Messrs

Fox cellars which adjoined the new lifeboat house.[3]

The first time the new lifeboat was launched for a rescue a huge wave thrust it back on shore. The boat was relaunched and with the crew valiantly rowing into the teeth of a near Force 10 gale, they reached the wreck, a schooner from Bordeaux, and successfully took off the crew. The fierce winds prevented them from entering Mevagissey harbour but they eventually managed to land on Par sands, soaked to the skin and utterly exhausted.[5]

Walter was grandfather to an increasing number of children. His oldest daughter Jane, following local custom, called her second son Walter after her father and her second daughter Ann, after her mother. Walter Pearce, known as 'Wall', became a popular Wesleyan preacher. Of Walter Williams' other daughters, Anne and Sophia married in 1870, and Elizabeth in 1871, and children soon followed. Walter's nephew Philip, who had, of course, served on the *Elizabeth Mary Ann* with his uncle, was awarded his master's certificate at Bristol in 1861 when he was 26. From 1861 to 1870 he was the master of the *Ganges*, a barque of 300 tons which sailed regularly from her home port of Newport to South America. Walter junior became a master in 1873, aged 25, and soon transferred from sailing vessels to the new steam ships, working mainly for the Liverpool firm of C.T. Bowring. His first ship as captain was the 640 ton *Romeo*, which had been built in Liverpool in 1869 and was owned by Bowrings. It traded between Liverpool and Australia. His father will have watched with interest, and perhaps some sadness, as steam replaced sail in the merchant navy. He may have felt some relief that he never had to cope with the smelly engines and the huge crews that the 'damned sea kettles' required to function. The trend for Mevagissey mariners to work more and more away from home, on ships registered in the expanding ports of Liverpool, Newcastle, Hull and London, continued as fewer and fewer sailing ships traded from Cornish ports.

As well as competition from steam ships there was competition from the railways, which had reached Cornwall in 1859 across Brunel's great bridge at Saltash, and were carrying an increasing quantity of goods. A station opened at St Austell on 4 May 1859 and, as well as passengers, the trains carried china clay from the St Austell area and fish from Mevagissey. The *West Briton* newspaper reported on 14 February 1871 that only two cargoes of pilchards had been sent

Grace Williams

from Cornwall to the Mediterranean by sailing vessels in the previous year; one, the *Racer*, had sailed from St Ives to Genoa in the remarkably quick time of fourteen days, while the *Maria Louise* of Charlestown took the same time from Newquay to Naples. There were some exceptions to the decline of the trading sailing ship in the area; the Stephens fleet of 'Little' ships was founded by John Stephens in Fowey in 1867, was at its zenith in 1902, with 17 vessels averaging 130 tons, and only ceased trading in 1939.[6]

It was quite a surprise to find out that Walter remarried on 24 January 1871. His bride, Grace Lanyon of Gorran, was 53, twelve years younger than her husband. Her family were farmers and she had been born at Trevascus Farm in Gorran, the oldest in a family of eight children. Her father, Robert, had died young in 1831, and her mother, also Grace, had carried on the farm with the help of her children until she died in 1860. Her oldest son, Robert, Grace's brother, took on the much larger farm at Treveague, also in Gorran, which is now a caravan park.

Mevagissey had changed a great deal since the day in 1839 that Walter had first sailed out of the harbour in the *Brilliant*. The local ship-building industry had been in decline for many years and only four new ships were built, all by the Lelean brothers, after 1850. However, the yards were still kept busy building fishing boats and carrying out repairs. In 1866 an Act of Parliament was obtained to allow the enlargement of the harbour. A new outer pier and basin and the Watch Tower were added and the overall harbour area increased from three acres to ten. The main quay was repaired and extended and additional buildings provided, including fish stores, corn stores and a new sail loft for the flourishing Lelean family sail-making business. The fishing industry, too, had changed over the years. In 1867 there were only two seines left in the harbour but by 1881 there were over 60 drift fishing boats. The drift fishing boats were larger and able to fish further out to sea for mackerel and herrings.

As well as opening up opportunities for trade in fishing, agriculture and china clay the arrival of the railway also stimulated the growth of tourism. In the mid-eighteenth century an attempt had been made to turn Mevagissey into a spa town. A bath surrounding a sulphurous (and foul-smelling) spring in the Treleaven valley was housed in a Greek-style temple and advertised as 'Equal and better than now advertised at the Pantiles, in Royal Tunbridge Wells'. The venture was not a success. Nevertheless, an increasing number of intrepid travellers, particularly artists or writers, visited Cornwall to rhapsodise about (or sometimes denigrate) the scenery and the natives. Tennyson visited Tintagel in 1842 and the visit is said to have inspired him to write *Morte D'Arthur*. In 1860 he accompanied his friend Palgrave on a walking holiday to Cornwall and as they walked they planned a collection of English poems which became the famous *Palgrave's Golden Treasury*. Tennyson's great fame and love of Cornwall must have inspired Walter's oldest daughter, Jane, to baptise her fourth son Alfred Tennyson Pearce on 3 May 1877. 'Ten', as he was always known, became a farmer and had one son, William, who helped me a great deal in the early stages of my research. He was the only surviving

Mevagissey harbour with the Lelean sail business in the background

The Jago monument in Mevagissey churchyard

relative of my mother's generation and had inherited a huge number of photographs from Great-Aunt Annie and other relatives. Sadly, he died in 2005.

Once the railway reached St Austell the number of visitors travelling to Mevagissey and Portmellon greatly increased. People came to enjoy the scenery, to go out fishing with the local fishermen, to paint the bustling harbour and to swim in the sea. The railway was also a great convenience for those who wished to travel away from Cornwall. Instead of enduring a long sea passage, probably combined with a lengthy coach journey, Mevagissey people travelling to London only had to go the 5 miles to St Austell to catch a train. Shortly after their marriage Walter and Grace went to London and stayed in Clapton. While they were there they visited the local photographers and had their pictures taken to commemorate their marriage. Walter, his beard tidily trimmed, still looks the shrewd, commanding but genial sea captain whilst Grace looks an intelligent and capable new wife for his life on land.

Grace and Walter enjoyed just over ten years of married life together. They lived alone at the Anchorage with no servants. On 24 March 1882 Walter's oldest daughter, Jane, gave birth to her seventh and last child, Tom. His grandfather will have only known him as a very young baby because on 21 October 1882 Walter died, according to the death certificate of 'paralysis'; presumably a stroke. He was 76. The decision was taken by his family to bury him in Mevagissey churchyard with his first wife, Ann. They were later joined by their youngest child, Sophia, when she died, aged only 42, in 1892.

Walter may have prospered and built himself a fine house but when he died he was not a very rich man. His estate was valued for probate at £582 16s. 6d. (£42,068 in 2007 based on the retail price index ).[7] The executors of his will were his two sons-in-law William Pearce (Jane's husband) and Samuel Trescott (Elizabeth's husband). He left the Anchorage and his furniture to his children with the provision that Grace could continue to live there for three months after his death. He also left her the Rock House, which was just down the road in Portmellon. Grace lived for another sixteen years and when she died on 10 December 1898 she was buried alone in Gorran churchyard.

Mevagissey parish church, St Peter's, was energetically restored by Piers St Aubyn in 1887. The churchyard, however, remains much as it was in the summer of 1849 when every day another two or three cholera victims were carried up from the town and buried without headstones. Wandering around it today one meets again those who lived in Mevagissey in the nineteenth century and whose names have appeared in this narrative. There are the monuments to the Jago family, a large grave for the Leleans and stones commemorating the Balls, the Pearces, the Allens, the Leys, the Dunns, the Behennas and the Rollings. Often the gravestones of members of the same family are grouped together. When I visited the churchyard again recently the great beech tree under which I had originally found Walter Williams' grave had been felled and some of the romance of the site had vanished with it. What I had failed to notice before, however, was that alongside the Williams gravestone there were three more stones, forming a close line rather like houses along a street. The first gravestone was in memory of Elizabeth Allen, Ann's mother, and the next to that most famous smuggler and ship-builder, James Dunn, who had died in 1842 aged 88. Carved on his gravestone are the dates that his wife and their 9

The Williams head-stone is on the left and the Dunn one on the right in Mevagissey church-yard

children died and their ages at death. One of these, of course, was Walter Dunn, the builder of the *Brilliant*, who had died in the 1849 cholera epidemic. It seemed appropriate that these people, who had known each other so intimately, should rest together just up the hill from the hustle and bustle of Mevagissey harbour which had been the centre of their working and family lives. They had all been a part of the flourishing trade in shipping and fish and other, sometimes less legal, goods which had been an essential part of the economy of the area.

'A Lelean could never be another man's servant,' wrote the Lelean family historian, and neither, I feel sure, could Walter Williams or any of the other master mariners from Mevagissey. Walter was a Mevagissey man and a Cornishman to the core; tough, resourceful, independent and ambitious. He was lucky to have begun his sailing career at a time when the carrying of freight all over the world in sailing ships was at its peak. By the time he died in 1882 that kind of life had almost disappeared. The remote, cliff-bound ports of the south-west could not compete with the fast-growing docks of Liverpool, London, Glasgow and the Tyne. Economic, geographical and technological developments meant that the men who built the ships and sailed the vessels had to adapt to the new conditions by finding new work locally or by migrating to these places.

The painting of the *Brilliant*, I had discovered, represented much more than mere romance and adventure; it was, and is, a symbol of a courageous enterprise that involved not just a few individuals but whole communities: the merchants who provided the capital, the goods and the organisation; the fishermen who caught at least some of the cargoes; the shipwrights, sawyers and carpenters who built the ships; the rope makers, block makers, blacksmiths and sail makers who supplied the materials for fitting out the ships. The painting of the *Brilliant* symbolises the end, not only of the great era of the merchant sailing vessels, but of a way of life for the coastal communities of Cornwall.

S. S. "JULIET," of Liverpool,

2030 Tons.

WALTER WILLIAMS, Commander.

The crew of the *S.S. Juliet* in New York, May 1883. The commander, Walter Williams junior, is standing on the left on the upper level

# THE INHERITANCE

**M**Y RESEARCH for this book had provided a context for the painting of the *Brilliant* and most of the objects that I, and other descendants of Captain Williams, have inherited. But the ship's model remained a mystery.

After his father's death Walter Williams junior continued to work on ships belonging to the Bowring Line. He was the master of the company's first steam sailing ship and in 1883 he was made the Commander of the *S.S. Juliet*, a large screw steam ship of 2,080 tons with a crew of 23. The *Juliet* had been built in Manchester in 1881 and had a very short life as she was wrecked on a voyage from Cardiff to New Orleans in 1886. Walter Williams was not her Commander on that voyage. The Bowring line was typical of the new kind of ship's company that developed in the larger ports in the nineteenth century. The Company was founded in St John's, Newfoundland in the 1820s by Benjamin Bowring, a clock maker from Devon, who built up a fleet

Model of a steam sailing ship made by Walter Williams junior

of small sailing ships specialising in the seal trade. In the 1840s his son, Charles Tricks Bowring, expanded the business, moving to Liverpool, and from the 1880s built up a fleet of ocean-going steam ships. I searched for references to the Bowring business on the internet and quickly discovered that the Bowring funnel was black with a broad band of white with a red St Andrew's cross.

Another mystery was solved. The ship's model has exactly this type of funnel markings. But it was a steam

sailing ship so could not have been the *Juliet*; it must have been one of the earlier ships that Walter Williams junior sailed in for the Bowrings. I presume that Walter junior had made the model himself, perhaps in the long days of retirement, for he was already retired at 45. He kept a boat moored at Portmellon and loved to go fishing although, like my mother, he hated fish.

Philip Williams, Walter senior's nephew, was still working at sea in 1891. His four sons, Albert, Philip, Joseph and Walter, who were living at home, were all mariners.

One other member of the family, my mother's brother, Thirlby, became a master mariner. His mother did not want her only son to go to sea and, hoping to deter him, she took him to Chapel Point to see a ship that had just been torpedoed and was on fire and sinking. This exciting sight only increased his determination and with the help of a family friend, Captain Pollard, he was apprenticed aboard the *Courtown* in October 1918 when he was 15. In 1927 he received his certificate of competency as a master of a foreign going ship. He travelled to many exotic places before settling in Port Sudan where he worked as a pilot. In 1931 he left the sea to marry Ida Wakelin. They had six children and he became a highly successful businessman.

The houses associated with Walter Williams and his family have almost all been taken over by the current major local industry – tourism. Only Trelawney, the house that my grandfather built up Tregoney Hill, is still just a home. Tregerrick, the Gorran farm belonging to Walter's eldest daughter, Jane and the Pearce family, is a B & B establishment. The Anchorage, perched perilously on the cliff at Portmellon, where Walter senior spent his retirement and where Walter junior lived, was brought back into the family in the 1960s when Sam Allen (see the family tree) bought it. Now the Anchorage is also a B & B and over the last few years I have been able to spend many happy hours there in the course of my research, listening to the sea from my bedroom and being spoilt with mouth-watering breakfasts by the present owners.

The smell of fish and chips now dominates the area around Mevagissey harbour and signs warn the tourists not to feed the predatory gulls. The local fishing

Portmellon 1930. Colona was built in front of the Anchorage in 1894 by the local journalist J. H. Harris. © The Francis Frith Collection

fleet has not completely disappeared; indeed it seems to be experiencing something of a revival, with a stall on the harbour selling fresh-caught fish and local restaurants advertising local catches. It is ironic that in the new, global economy the home market has become the main market for most of the fish caught by Mevagissey fishermen. In the 1890s a factory for canning and preserving pilchards was established in the town and for many people in the twentieth century the pilchard has been known only as something to be bought in a flat tin: a small fish imbedded in gooey tomato sauce. However, in 1997 the fish was re-branded as a 'Cornish sardine' (a sardine is a young pilchard) with some success, particularly amongst the increasing number of people who enjoy cooking on barbecues. Currently, the 'specialties' on the menu at the Rising Sun Inn in Portmellon include 'chargrilled fresh Cornish sardines'. I suspect that if Captain Walter Langford Williams were alive he might be doing exactly what Dermot and Pat, the current owners of the Anchorage, are doing – running a very superior bed and breakfast establishment in a uniquely beautiful part of the country and perhaps even serving 'Cornish sardines' for dinner.

# FAMILY TREES

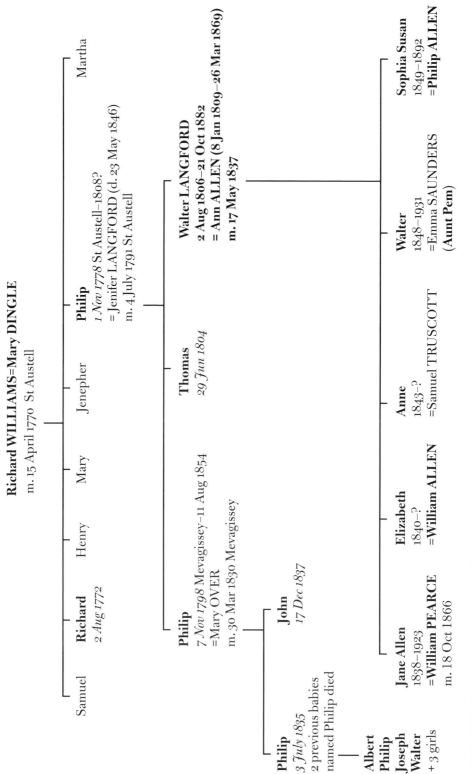

**The family of WALTER LANGFORD WILLIAMS (1806–1882)**

**Richard WILLIAMS=Mary DINGLE**
m. 15 April 1770  St Austell

Samuel    **Richard**
          *2 Aug 1772*

Henry    Mary    Jenepher    **Philip**
                             *1 Nov 1778* St Austell–1808?
                             =Jenifer LANGFORD (d. 23 May 1846)
                             m. 4 July 1791 St Austell

**Philip**
*7 Nov 1798* Mevagissey–11 Aug 1854
=Mary OVER
m. 30 Mar 1830 Mevagissey

**Thomas**
*29 Jun 1804*

Martha

**Walter LANGFORD**
*2 Aug 1806–21 Oct 1882*
= Ann ALLEN (8 Jan 1809–26 Mar 1869)
**m. 17 May 1837**

**Philip**
*3 July 1835*
2 previous babies
named Philip died

**John**
*17 Dec 1837*

**Albert
Philip
Joseph
Walter**
+ 3 girls

**Jane Allen**
1838–1923
=**William PEARCE**
m. 18 Oct 1866

**Elizabeth**
1840–?
=**William ALLEN**

**Anne**
1843–?
=Samuel TRUSCOTT

**Walter**
1848–1931
=Emma SAUNDERS
(**Aunt Pem**)

**Sophia Susan**
1849–1892
=**Philip ALLEN**

*ITALICS indicate date of baptism not birth*
**Bold** type indicates people mentioned in text.

**Descendants of Jane Allen Williams, oldest child of Walter Langford Williams**

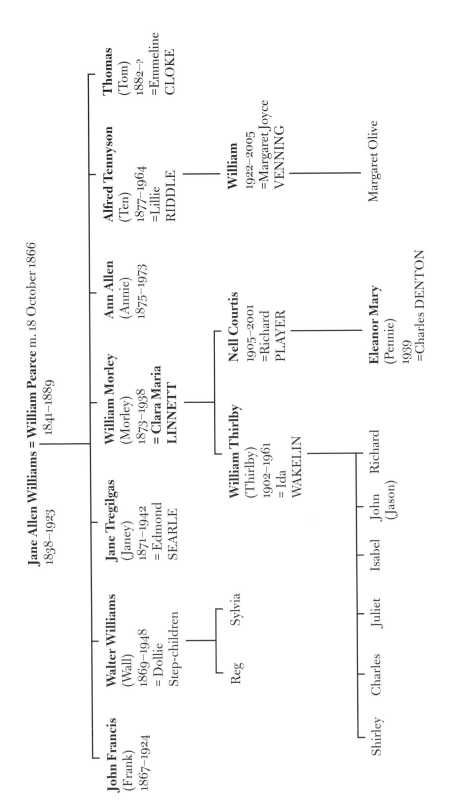

**Jane Allen Williams** = **William Pearce** m. 18 October 1866
1838–1923                                          1841–1889

**John Francis**
(Frank)
1867–1924

**Walter Williams**
(Wall)
1869–1948
= Dollie
Step-children

Reg        Sylvia

**Jane Tregilgas**
(Janey)
1871–1942
= Edmond
SEARLE

**William Morley**
(Morley)
1873–1938
= **Clara Maria
LINNETT**

**William Thirlby**
(Thirlby)
1902–1961
= Ida
WAKELIN

Shirley    Charles    Juliet    Isabel    John    Richard
                                                (Jason)

**Nell Courtis**
1905–2001
= Richard
PLAYER

**Eleanor Mary**
(Pennie)
1939
= Charles DENTON

**Ann Allen**
(Annie)
1875–1973

**Alfred Tennyson**
(Ten)
1877–1964
= Lillie
RIDDLE

**William**
1922–2005
= Margaret Joyce
VENNING

Margaret Olive

**Thomas**
(Tom)
1882–?
= Emmeline
CLOKE

# Descendants of Sophia Susan Williams, youngest child of Walter Langford Williams

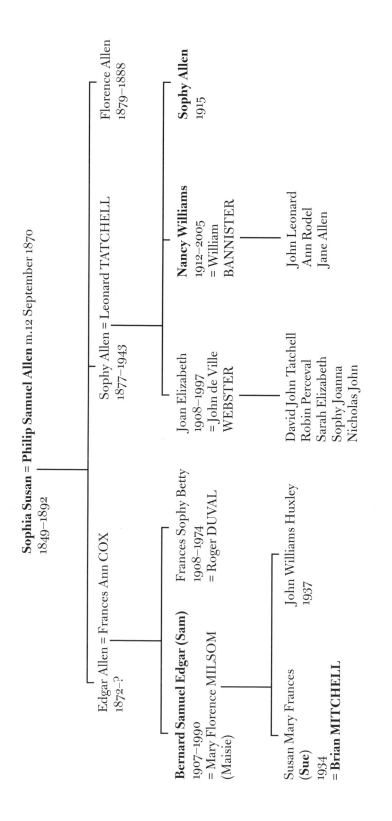

**Sophia Susan** = **Philip Samuel Allen** m.12 September 1870
1849–1892

Edgar Allen = Frances Ann COX
1872–?

Sophy Allen = Leonard TATCHELL
1877–1943

Florence Allen
1879–1888

**Bernard Samuel Edgar (Sam)**
1907–1990
= Mary Florence MILSOM
(Maisie)

Frances Sophy Betty
1908–1974
= Roger DUVAL

Joan Elizabeth
1908–1997
= John de Ville
WEBSTER

**Nancy Williams**
1912–2005
= William
BANNISTER

**Sophy Allen**
1915

Susan Mary Frances
(**Sue**)
1934
= **Brian MITCHELL**

John Williams Huxley
1937

David John Tatchell
Robin Perceval
Sarah Elizabeth
Sophy Joanna
Nicholas John

John Leonard
Ann Rodel
Jane Allen

# ACKNOWLEDGEMENTS

I am but one of a large number of descendants of Captain Walter Langford Williams, many of whom have helped me with my researches into his life. First on my list to thank must be William Pearce, a cousin of my mother's and one of the few descendants who lived all his life in Cornwall. As the guardian of the family Bible and Great-Aunt Annie's photograph collection, he was ever generous with his time and, with his daughter Margaret and her family, traditional Cornish hospitality. Sadly he died in 2005. I am grateful to Sue (née Allen) and Brian Mitchell, who live in Mevagissey and were able to tell me a great deal about the Anchorage, where Sue's family had lived, and about the area. It was fascinating to hear from Brian about the more recent history of boatbuilding in Portmellon from someone who had himself built boats there with his father, Percy Mitchell, and his brother. I am also grateful to Sue's brother, John Allen, who looks after the Allen family photographs and kindly arranged for me to have copies or borrow the originals and to my cousin Richard Pearce who, at the last minute, sent me fascinating information about his father, Thirlby, only a small part of which I could include. Nancy Bannister, who died in 2005, and her sister, Sophy Tatchell, recalled anecdotes of Captain Williams and had their own memories of his son, also Captain Walter Williams, who they knew well. I thank them both for their time and for the fun we had recalling our interesting, and sometimes eccentric, ancestors.

I am grateful to Sir Arthur Quiller Couch Memorial Fund (which is administered by Cornwall County Council) for the grant I received to help illustrate the book.

In the field of maritime history I owe a great debt to Helen Doe, whose course at Exeter University *The Lost World of the Sailing Ships* I took in 2006. Staff at the Cornwall Centre, the Cornwall Record Office, the National Archives, National Maritime Museum, the Guildhall Library, the Merseyside Maritime Museum and Mevagissey Museum helped me find the most relevant local history and maritime records and Angela Broome, the marvellous librarian at the Courtney Library at the Royal Institution of Cornwall showed me the rich material on Mevagissey collected by the Reverend Mapplebeck and Frank Baron. At the Courtney Photographic Library Rob Cook showed skill in finding the images I was seeking.

Thank you to Dr James Whetter for allowing me to use the quotation on page 84, to Jonathan Varcoe, Grace White, Dermot and Pat Lee, Sally and Tim Kendall and Charles Denton, my ever-patient and resourceful husband.

Finally, thank you to Roger Hudson and Susanna Powers for editorial help, to Adrian Bartlett for designing the map on page 4, Carlotta Barrow for photographic work and to Sheri Gee for the design and production of the book.

# NOTES

NA – National Archives, Kew
    BT – Board of Trade: Registrar General of Seamen Agreements and Crew Lists
    C – Chancery
    FO – Foreign Office
CRO – Cornwall Record Office, Truro
RCM CL – Royal Cornwall Museum, Courtney Library, Truro
NMM – National Maritime Museum
MMM MAL – Merseyside Maritime Museum, Maritime Archive and Library

## INTRODUCTION

1. Gray, Todd (ed.) *Cornwall: The Travellers' Tales*. Exeter: The Mint Press, 2000. p. 72.

## CHAPTER 1: THE SEARCH

1. Seal, Jeremy. *The Wreck at Sharpnose Point: A Victorian Mystery*. London: Picador, 2003. p. 269.

## CHAPTER 2: PILCHARDS AND PROSPERITY

1. Harris, J.H. 'Some Notes on Old Mevagissey' in *Royal Institution of Cornwall Journal*, Volume xix, Part 3, 1914. p. 356.
2. Gray, Todd (ed.) *Cornwall: The Travellers' Tales*. Exeter: The Mint Press, 2000. p. 38.
3. Hamilton Jenkins, A.K. *Cornwall and its People*. Newton Abbott: David and Charles, pb. ed. 1988 (1st ed. 1945). p. 92.
4. Noall, Cyril. *Cornish Seines and Seiners. A History of the Pilchard Fishing Industry*. Truro: Bradford Barton, 1972. p. 42.
5. Ibid. pp. 50–1.
6. RCM CL. Mapplebeck Collection. File 8/5.
7. Harris, J.H. op. cit. pp. 355–6.
8. Pearse, Richard. *The Ports and Harbours of Cornwall: An Introduction to the Study of 800 years of Maritime History*. St Austell: H.E. Warne Ltd., 1964. p. 57.
9. Brett, R.L.(ed.) *Barclay Fox's Journal*. London: Bell & Hyman, 1979. p. 160.

1. Dunn, Matthias. 'Men of Mevagissey' in *Old Cornwall*, Volume 3, 1937–42. p. 293.
2. Ibid. p. 294.
3. Ward-Jackson, C.H. *Ships and Shipbuilders of a Westcountry Seaport; Fowey 1786–1939.* Truro: Twelveheads Press, 1986. p. 106.
4. Ibid. pp. 14–15.
5. Waugh, Mary. *Smuggling in Devon and Cornwall, 1700–1850.* Newbury: Countryside Books, 1991. p. 141.
6. *West Briton.* 7 August 1835.
7. RCM CL. Furse, Thomas. *Family Memoirs: The Life of Thomas Furse 1767–1838.* Typed transcript, p. 14.
8. CRO MSR/FOW/1. *Port of Fowey Ship Registers.*
9. CRO MSR/FOW/1/1798/2. *Port of Fowey Ship Registers.*
10. NA C110/167. *Dunn & Henna shipbuilders Accounts and inventories 1799–1815.*
11. CRO MSR/FOW/1/1803/22. *Port of Fowey Ship Registers.*
12. Doe, Helen. *Small Shipbuilding Businesses During the Napoleonic Wars: James Dunn of Mevagissey, 1799–1816.* Unpublished thesis for Master of Arts degree, University of Exeter, 2003.
13. Johns, Jeremy Rowett. *The Smugglers' Banker. The Story of Zephaniah Job of Polperro.* Liskeard: Polperro Heritage Press, 1997. p. 136.

## CHAPTER 4: GROWING UP IN MEVAGISSEY

1. Mevagissey Museum. *The History of Mevagissey*, n.d. p. 5.
2. Murrish, Robert. *A History of Mevagissey Methodists, 1752–1980.* 1980. p. 9.
3. Ibid. Appendix, pp. 1–6.
4. Behenna, H.A. *A Cornish Harbour.* H.A. Behenna, 1995. p. 18.
5. Ibid. p. 19.
6. Murrish, Robert. op cit. pp. 3–4.
7. Samuel Dunn. *Memoirs of Mr. Joseph Allen of Mevagissey, Cornwall.* London: Simpkin, Marshal & Co., 1838. p. 1.
8. Hamilton Jenkins, A.K. op cit. p. 186.
9. Harris, T. R. *Samuel Dunn 1798–1882. Reformer.* Redruth: Cornish Methodist Historical Association, 1963.
10. Mevagissey Museum. op. cit. p. 8.
11. Roberts, J. Kitto. *The Mevagissey Independents, 1625–1946.* Raunton: F. Goodman & Son, Ltd., 1946. p. 24.
12. *West Briton.* 14 November 1825.

1. NMM, *Master's Claim for Certificate of Service 24 March 1851*. Walter Williams.
2. NA BT98/264. *Registrar General of Shipping and Seamen, Agreements, Crew Lists and Official Logs. Fowey*. Susanna. 1 July–31 December 1835.
3. Ward-Jackson, C.H. op. cit. p. 13.
4. CRO MSR/FOW/2/1830/Susanna. *Port of Fowey Ships Registers*.
5. Ward-Jackson, C. H. op. cit. p. 32.
6. Behenna, R.B.(ed.) *A Victorian Sailor's Diary. Richard Behenna of Veryan, 1833–1898*. Redruth: Institute of Cornish Studies, 1981. p. 11.
7. Ibid. p. 14.
8. *West Briton*. 24 March 1826.

1. Mitchell, Percy. *A Boatbuilder's Story*. Mevagissey: Kingston, 1968. p. 20.
2. Doe, Helen. op. cit. pp. 6–74.
3. Greenhill, Basil. *The Merchant Schooners*. Newton Abbot, 1968 (first ed. 1951), p. 27.
4. Greenhill, Basil. *The Merchant Schooners*. London: Conway Maritime Press, 1988. p. 67.
5. NA C110/167. *Dunn & Henna Shipbuilders Accounts and Inventories 1799–1815*.
6. Doe, Helen. op. cit.
7. CRO MSR/FOW/3/1839/3/Brilliant. *Port of Fowey Ships Registers*.

1. Greenhill, Basil. *The Merchant Schooners*. London: Conway, 1988. p. 120.
2. NA BT98/262. *Registrar General of Shipping and Seamen, Agreements, Crew Lists and Official Logs. Fowey*. Brilliant. March 1839.
3. NA BT98/1224. *Registrar General of Shipping and Seamen, Agreements, Crew Lists and Official Logs. Fowey*. Brilliant. May–October 1847.
4. NA BT98/262. *Registrar General of Shipping and Seamen, Agreements, Crew Lists and Official Logs. Fowey*. Brilliant. 26 September 1839.
5. NA BT98/262. *Registrar General of Shipping and Seamen, Agreements, Crew Lists and Official Logs. Fowey*. Brilliant. 23 October 1839 – 15 February 1840.

### CHAPTER 8: CORNOVAGLIA–NAPOLI

1. Noall, Cyril. op. cit. p. 51.
2. *Lloyd's List.* 16 November 1839.
3. RCM CL. *Baron 1/11. Mevagissey Quay accounts*, October 1844.
4. Trevelyan, Raleigh. *Princes Under the Volcano. Two Hundred Years of a British Dynasty in Sicily.* London: Phoenix Press, 2002 (1st ed. 1972).
5. NA FO354/16. *Woodbine Parish Papers*, 1844–46.
6. *Lloyd's List.* 2 Jan 1840, 15 Feb 1840.
7. MMM MAL. *Customs Bill of Entry, Liverpool.* 27 December 1841.

### CHAPTER 9: HOME AND AWAY

1. *Lloyd's List.* Dates as shown in text.
2. Internet. *Will of Elizabeth Hicks*, June 1843.
3. CRO ACP/WILLS/W/1846. *Will of Jane Williams*, 6 July 1846.
4. http://www.gorran-haven.com/lelean
5. *Lloyd's List.* 18 Dec 1847.
6. NA BT98/1576. *Registrar General of Shipping and Seamen, Agreements, Crew Lists and Official Logs. Fowey.* Brilliant. August 1848.
7. *Royal Cornwall Gazette.* 22 December 1848. p. 2.

### CHAPTER 10: A DEADLY FOE

1. Rowe, John. *Cornwall in the Age of the Industrial Revolution.* St Austell, Cornish Hillside Publications, 1993. p. 30.
2. NA BT127. *Index to Registers of Certificates of Competency and Service, Masters and Mates, Home and Foreign Trade* (1845–1894).
3. Ward-Jackson, C. H. op. cit. p. 39.
4. *Lloyd's List.* 1 Dec 1849.
5. Bouquet, Michael. 'Passengers from Torquay: Emigration to North America, 1849–1859' in Fisher, H.E.S. (ed.) *Ports and Shipping in the South-West.* Exeter: Exeter University Press, 1971.
6. MMM MAL. *Customs Bill of Entry, Liverpool.* 30 Sept 1850.
7. *Royal Cornwall Gazette.* 24 November 1854. p. 5.
8. Ward-Jackson, C. H. op. cit. p. 34.

### CHAPTER 11: KING CHOLERA

1. Mevagissey Museum. op. cit. p. 9.
2. *West Briton*, 24 August 1849.
3. Mevagissey Museum. op cit. p. 9.

4. Murrish, Robert C. op. cit. p. 21.
5. RCM CL. Mapplebeck Collection, File 8/5.
6. Kingsley, Charles. *The Waters of Life and other Sermons. Sermon XVII, Cholera, 1866*. London: Macmillan, 1881.
7. Murrish, Robert C. op. cit. p. 21.
8. Longmate, Norman. *King Cholera: The Biography of a Disease*. London: Hamish Hamilton, 1966. p. 1.
9. Avery, John G. *The Cholera Years*. Southampton: Beech Books, 2001. pp. 92 & 99.

### CHAPTER 12: A MERCHANT AND A GENTLEMAN

1. NA WILLS/B11/2000. *Will of John Pearce*, 25 June 1844.
2. Brett, R.L. op. cit. p. 162.
3. Brett, R.L. op. cit. p. 84.
4. NA WILLS/B11/2118. *Will of John Pearce*, 12 August 1850.

### CHAPTER 13: A DAM BAD OLD MAN

1. Course, A. *The Merchant Navy: A Social History*. London: Frederick Muller, 1963. pp. 195–6.
2. Ibid. pp. 207–8.
3. NA BT98/3338. NA BT98/262. *Registrar General of Shipping and Seamen, Agreements, Crew Lists and Official Logs. Fowey*. Elizabeth Mary Ann. September 1853.
4. *Lloyd's List*. 25 September 1853.
5. NA BT98/3736 NA. *Registrar General of Shipping and Seamen, Agreements, Crew Lists and Official Logs. Fowey*. Elizabeth Mary Ann. April 1854.
6. NA BT98/5491. *Registrar General of Shipping and Seamen, Agreements, Crew Lists and Official Logs. Fowey*. Elizabeth Mary Ann. September 1858.

### CHAPTER 14: ILLNESS AND DISEASE

1. Kerndal, Roald. *Seamen's Missions*. California: William Carey Library, 1986. p. 55.
2. Course, A. op cit. p. 195.
3. NA BT98/4015. *Registrar General of Shipping and Seamen, Agreements, Crew Lists and Official Logs. Truro*. Kate. February–May 1854.
4. NA BT98/3904. *Registrar General of Shipping and Seamen, Agreements, Crew Lists and Official Logs. Milford Haven*. D'Israeli. May–November 1854.
5. Bullen, Frank. *The Log of a Sea-Waif*. New York: Appleton, 1899.
6. RCM CL. Furse, Thomas. op cit. p. 14.

7. CRO ACP/WILLS/L. *Will of Thomas Ley.* 18 April 1856.

8. NA BT98/6880. *Registrar General of Shipping and Seamen, Agreements, Crew Lists and Official Logs. Fowey.* Elizabeth Mary Ann. September 1859.

CHAPTER 15: ELIZABETH MARY ANN

1. Marquand, Hilary. *Memoirs of a Victorian Master Mariner.* Cardiff: Merton Priory Press, 1996. pp. 231–6.

2. CRO MSR/FOW/3/1872. *Port of Fowey Ship Registers.* Elizabeth Mary Ann.

3. Craig, Greenhill, Porter & Slade. 'Some Aspects of the Business of Devon Shipping in the 19th century' in Duffy et al. (eds.) *A New Maritime History of Devon.* London: Conway, 1994. pp. 99–100.

4. Kennett, D.H. 'The *Magic*: A Westcountry Schooner in the Mediterranean, 1833–39' in Fisher, H. E. S. (ed.) *West Country Maritime and Social History: Some Essays.* Exeter: Exeter University Press, 1980.p. 123.

5. Ward-Jackson, C.H. op. cit. Appendix 'I', pp. 110–113.

6. MMM MAL. *Bill of Entry, Liverpool.* 3 Aug 1848 and 28 Oct 1861.

7. *Lloyd's List.* 28 Jan 1856.

8. *Lloyd's List.* 3 May 1856.

9. MMM MAL. *Ships Loading, Liverpool.* 16 Aug 1864.

10. MMM MAL. *Bill of Entry, Liverpool.* 8 Jan 1855.

11. Pease, R. 'The Batten Castle: The Account Book of a Small Home Trade Sailing Vessel, 1852–1866' in Fisher, H. E. S. op. cit. p. 133.

12. Murch, D.F. 'Trading Vessels of Salcombe Haven, 1820–1890' in Fisher, H.E.S. *Ports and Shipping in the South-West.* Exeter: Exeter University Press, 1971. p. 125.

13. RCM CL. Mapplebeck Collection. File 1.

14. Craig, Greenhill, Porter & Slade. op. cit. p. 100.

15. http://www.measuringworth.com

16. Marquand, Hilary. op. cit. p. xxiii.

17. Craig, Robin S. 'Ship-owning in the South-West in its National Context, 1800–1914' in Fisher, H.E.S. & Minchinton, W.E. *Transport and Ship-owning in the West Country.* Exeter: Exeter University Press, 1973. p. 36.

CHAPTER 16: THE ANCHORAGE

1. NA BT98/3338. *Registrar General of Shipping and Seamen, Agreements, Crew Lists and Official Logs. Fowey.* Elizabeth Mary Ann, July–December 1865.

2. NA BT124/13. *Registers of Certificates of Service, Masters and Mates, Foreign Trade* (1850–1888).

3. RCM CL. Mapplebeck Collection. File 6/1.
4. Whetter, James. *Old Portmellon*. Gorran, Lyfrow Trelyspen, 2003. pp. 28–9.
5. Mevagissey Museum. op. cit. p. 10.
6. Ward-Jackson, C.H. op. cit. p. 70
7. http://www.measuringworth.com

# ILLUSTRATIONS

# INDEX

Illustrations shown in **bold**